GANDHI THE MAN

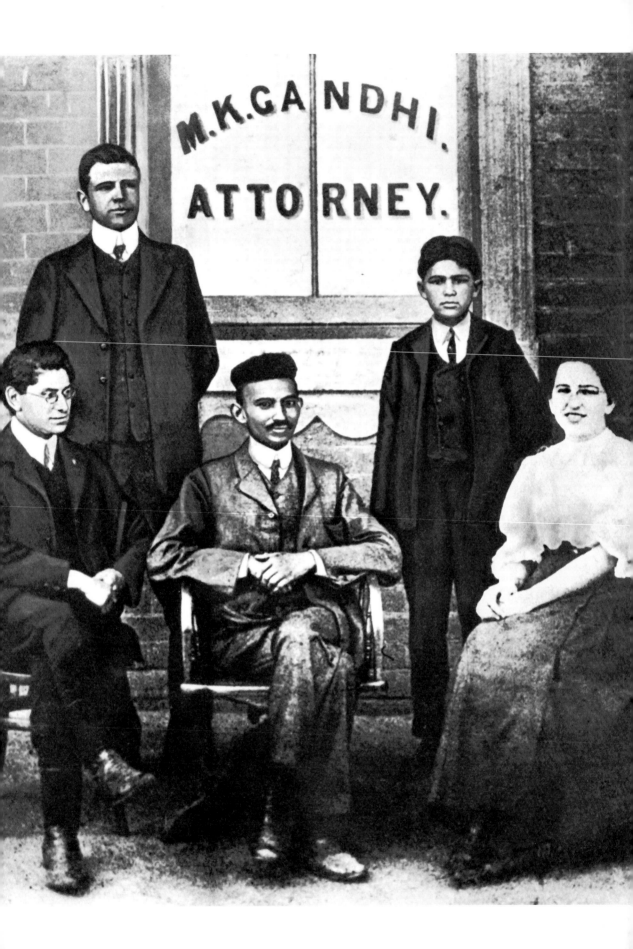

GANDHI THE MAN

The Story of His Transformation

by EKNATH EASWARAN

Foreword by Michael N. Nagler

Afterword by Timothy Flinders

NILGIRI PRESS

"I am not a visionary. I claim to be a practical idealist."

"I have not the shadow of a doubt than any man or woman can achieve what I have, if he or she would make the same effort and cultivate the same hope and faith."

Third edition 1997, second printing July 1998
Paperback I S B N 0–915132–96–6
Cloth I S B N 0–915132–97–4

Quotations from Gandhi are reprinted by kind permission of the
Navajivan Trust, Ahmedabad 14, India

The Blue Mountain Center of Meditation, founded in Berkeley,
California, in 1961 by Eknath Easwaran, publishes books on
how to lead the spiritual life in the home and the community.
For more information please write to
Nilgiri Press, Box 256, Tomales, California 94971

Printed on recycled, permanent paper

Library of Congress Cataloging-in-Publication Data:
Easwaran, Eknath
Gandhi the man : the story of his transformation /
by Eknath Easwaran; foreword by Michael N. Nagler;
afterword by Timothy Flinders. – 3rd. ed.
p. cm.
Includes bibliographical references and index.
I S B N 0–915132–97–4   I S B N 0–915132–96–6 (pbk.)
1. Gandhi, Mahatma, 1869–1948.
2. Statesmen– India–Biography.
I. Title
D S 481.G3 E19   1997
954.03′5′092–dc21
[B]   97–4662   CIP

Table of Contents

Foreword by Michael N. Nagler 5

THE TRANSFORMATION 11

THE WAY OF LOVE 41

MOTHER AND CHILD 105

GANDHI THE MAN 125

Appendix: HOW NONVIOLENCE WORKS 147

by Timothy Flinders

More about Gandhi and Ahimsa 172

Acknowledgments 174

Index 175

Foreword

"Historians of the future, I believe, will look upon this century not as the atomic age, but as the age of Gandhi."

When I first heard this statement it was 1966; the occasion was a talk on the campus of the University of California at Berkeley, given by a visiting scholar named Eknath Easwaran. I appreciated the sentiment, but it never occurred to me that the words were meant to be taken literally. Now I wonder. Every year, it seems, some prominent figure (one of the most significant being E. F. Schumacher) steps forward to acknowledge the light Gandhi shed on his or her field: economics, education, politics, philosophy, even diet and health. Social activists look on him as the father of nonviolence, and at least one of them, Dr. Martin Luther King, Jr., drew on his example to bring about profound and lasting changes in the social structure of our own country. And no less an observer than Lewis Mumford has called him "the most important religious figure of our time." Probably no one has summed it up better than the tireless American peace advocate Kirby Page, who by the time of his death in 1957 had met almost every prominent public figure to set foot on the stage of history in the twentieth century. "When I first wrote down my impressions," Page wrote, "the title of my little booklet ended with a question mark, *Is Mahatma Gandhi the Greatest Man of the Age?* Long since that question mark has been erased from my mind."

But the question how Gandhi achieved this greatness is still very much with us, and that is the most searching question of all. For each of these achievements represents only one part of the man, and no part of him can really be understood unless we first discover the man himself. "My life," Gandhi tells us, "is an indivisible whole, and all my activities run into one another...." Gandhi's real achievement lay not in any one field *per se,* but in the most important job that faces every man, woman, and child on earth: the job of living. How did he manage, as Easwaran puts it, to "make his life such a perfect work of art"? When we first get a glimpse of Gandhi he is a hapless, unprepossessing youth whose only distinction is a marked fear of the dark – and, as he loved to point out, his unusually large ears. How did he become a magnetic leader whom even his avowed opponents could not resist? How did this young man with the violent temper learn to sit cheerfully through all sorts of abusive criticism and emerge with his opponent treating him like a long-lost friend? How, in sum, did he manage to expand the narrow little personality of Mohandas K. Gandhi to become Mahatma, the immense force for human progress which has been described by countless biographers but accounted for by none?

Here is where the great advantage of an interpreter like Eknath Easwaran comes in. Easwaran was born in Gandhi's India, when it was still the crest jewel of the British Empire. His beautiful native village, like so many villages in South India, lay outside the mainstream of that political ferment which we regard as history. The major influence on his life was – and is – not the Gandhi who was remaking India, but the woman whom Easwaran regards as his spiritual teacher, his mother's mother: a simple woman of great spiritual stature, completely unknown to history, who never lived anywhere outside her ancestral village and certainly never participated in anything like a social movement. Her legacy to Easwaran was something that ran much deeper than the movement for India's independence: the rich spiritual tradition of Hinduism, probably over five thousand years old, whose highest ideals – nonviolence, love, and selfless service – she conveyed in her own daily example.

As Easwaran grew up, his life took him far beyond the physical and intellectual confines of his grandmother's world. He was a promising writer and a successful lecturer when he went to visit Gandhi, at the height of the movement for independence. But it was the spiritual tradition conveyed by his grandmother that enabled him to see beyond Gandhi the politician to Gandhi the man.

The story of Easwaran's meeting with Gandhi has left a deep impression on me. I can almost see the dusty plain of central India under the forbidding heat of the midafternoon sun when Easwaran walked the few miles from the train station at Wardha to the tiny collection of mud huts Gandhi had christened Sevagram, "village of service," from which he was patiently resurrecting a nation of four hundred million people. Easwaran spent the afternoon hours quietly observing, careful not to impose on anyone's time. Even then he must have been a somewhat different kind of pilgrim from those who characteristically gathered around Gandhi wherever he went. He had not come to observe Gandhi's political style or to satisfy his intellectual curiosity. Nor had he come, like the VIPs from Delhi, to get a decision on some weighty question of policy, or, like the innumerable common people who had equal access to Gandhi, to ask for personal advice. As a young man, Easwaran had watched other young men and women leave their studies to join Gandhi's work and had seen them transformed into heroes and heroines under the Mahatma's influence. "I wanted to know," Easwaran recalls simply, "the secret of his power."

In the prayer meeting that evening at Sevagram, Easwaran got his answer. Together with the rest of the ashram, he returned from the brisk after-dinner walk with Gandhi in the relative cool of the evening and settled down around the neem tree where Gandhi sat. Mahadev Desai, Gandhi's secretary, began to read out the verses from India's most treasured scripture, the Bhagavad Gita: "He lives in wisdom who sees himself in all and all in him, whose love for the Lord of Love has consumed every selfish desire and sense craving tormenting the heart. . . ." As Easwaran watched, the small brown body seated in front of him grew motionless, absorbed in meditation on those verses. "I was no longer hearing the Gita," Easwaran recalls; "I was *seeing* it, seeing the transformation it describes."

India is a land of wide contrasts but deep unity. The spiritual force Easwaran glimpsed that evening in Gandhi has surfaced countless times on the Indian subcontinent, and though the lives of those it changes may appear very different, the force itself is the same. Later, when Easwaran took to the practice of meditation in order to transform his own life, the model he strove to emulate was very much his grandmother. But it was from Gandhi, whose life was an open book, that he learned how to translate the highest ideal of mankind into everyday living. Gandhi was an inveterate tinkerer; in a country where the bonds of tradition have always been strong, he was making changes in his way of living, chipping away at imperfections, right up to the day he died. His manual for all this experimentation – his "spiritual reference book," as he called it – was the Bhagavad Gita, and Easwaran made it his manual too. For all their outward differences, both have used the Gita to shape their lives, and when Easwaran interprets Gandhi's transformation for us, it is with the authority of his own personal experience.

In courses I teach at the University of California I often make use of an excellent documentary called *Gandhi's India,* based on BBC interviews with many people who knew Gandhi or took part in his work. Among those interviewed is a woman named Asha Devi, who for my students and me is the star of the show. When she is asked, "What was Gandhi like? Describe the dominant impression he made on one," she sums up the secret of Gandhi the man in three words: "His great love." Then, a little later, the interviewer voices a doubt one often hears in connection with a person of Gandhi's stature: "Don't you think that he was a bit unrealistic, that he failed to reckon with the limits of our capacities?" It is hard to convey the joyful twinkle in Asha Devi's eyes as she answers, "There are no limits to our capacities."

It is the authentic voice of the Gita – or, for that matter, of the Bible or the Koran. Despite what we hear now from many scientists, we are not the product of our upbringing or our genes. As human beings, our greatness lies not so much in being able to remake the world outside us – that is the myth of the "atomic age" – as in being able to remake ourselves. We were all born for the glorious ideal of nonviolence and truth, and if we can catch fire from this ideal, there is no disadvantage that flesh is heir to that can prevent us from rising to our full human stature. That is what Asha Devi got from Gandhi, and that is what Easwaran has tried to convey in the pages that follow. I hope this new edition of *Gandhi the Man* will reach more readers who can say, as so many did of the first edition, "This book helped me to change my life."

—MICHAEL N. NAGLER *University of California, Berkeley*

The Transformation

There was nothing unusual about the boy Mohandas Karamchand Gandhi, except perhaps that he was very, very shy. He had no unusual talents, and went through school as a somewhat less than average student: self-conscious and serious, deeply devoted to his parents, and only vaguely aware of anything outside the quiet seaside town of his birth. It was the end of the nineteenth century, when the British Empire, at the peak of its wealth and power, extended around the world. India was in its second century of British domination.

"I was born at Porbandar, otherwise known as Sudamapuri, on the 2nd October, 1869. I passed my childhood at Porbandar. I recollect having been put to school. It was with some difficulty that I got through the multiplication tables. The fact that I recollect nothing more of those days than having learnt, in company with other boys, to call our teacher all kinds of names, would strongly suggest that my intellect must have been sluggish, and my memory raw."

Porbandar: the street
on which Gandhi
grew up.
(Courtesy Indian Opinion)

"I used to be very shy and avoided all company. My books and my lessons were my sole companions. To be at school at the stroke of the hour and to run back home as soon as the school closed – that was my daily habit. I literally ran back, because I could not bear to talk to anybody. I was even afraid lest anyone should poke fun at me."

"Moreover, I was a coward. I used to be haunted by the fear of thieves, ghosts, and serpents. I did not dare to stir out of doors at night. Darkness was a terror to me. It was almost impossible for me to sleep in the dark, as I would imagine ghosts coming from one direction, thieves from another and serpents from a third. I could not therefore bear to sleep without a light in the room."

Gandhi at age seven.

(Courtesy Jan Baros)

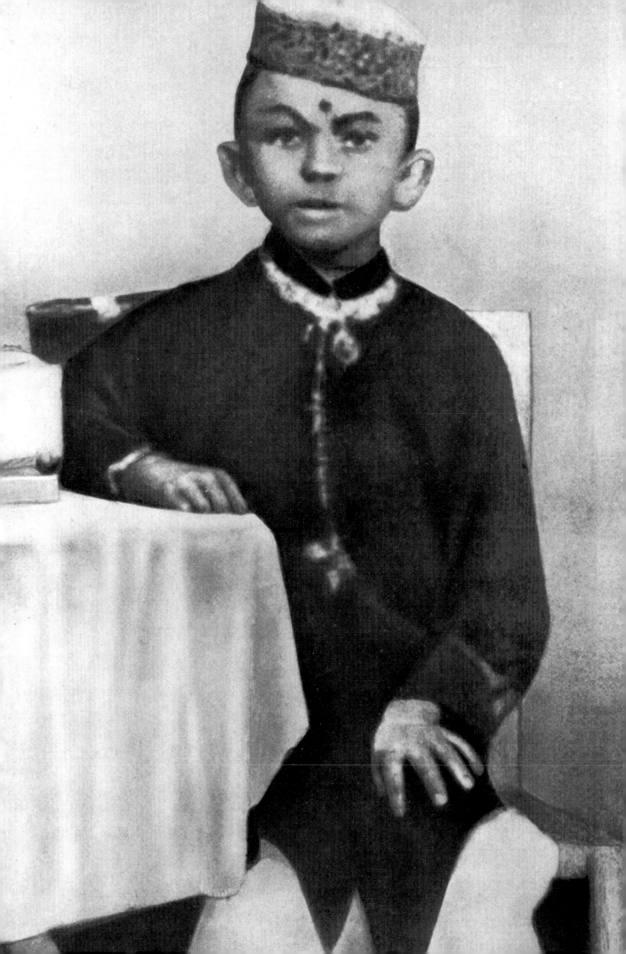

At the age of thirteen, while he was still in high school, Gandhi was married. It was, he wrote later, a "preposterously early" age. But Kasturbai was an attractive girl, and Gandhi quickly learned the role of a passionate, jealous, and exacting husband. Both children had a will and temper of their own, and the marriage had its stormy side from the start. In Gandhi's youthful mind, he was her teacher. Later he would realize that by her own forbearing example, it was she who had been teaching him. Her patience, her strength, her capacity to endure and forgive must have taken root deep within him during those early years, not to blossom until his campaigns in South Africa several years to come.

"I must say I was passionately fond of her. Even at school I used to think of her, and the thought of nightfall and our subsequent meeting was ever haunting me. Separation was unbearable. I used to keep her awake till late at night with my idle talk."

"How could I disclose my fears to my wife, no child, but already at the threshold of youth, sleeping by my side? I knew that she had more courage than I, and I felt ashamed of myself. She knew no fear of serpents and ghosts. She could go out anywhere in the dark."

Kasturbai Gandhi when she first arrived in South Africa in 1896, at the age of twenty-seven.
(From the film *Mahatma,* by permission of Vithalbhai K. Jhaveri)

Gandhi graduated from high school with a mediocre average and went doggedly on to college. He had some vague ambition to become a doctor, but it was never to be realized. He failed in every class. Each subject seemed impossible to follow, and he felt acutely out of place wherever he turned. After five months of consistent failure he withdrew from school and came back home. He had not the slightest idea of where to turn.

An uncle came to his rescue. Gandhi, he suggested, should go to London to study law. It took only three years to become a barrister, and a London degree in British India seemed certain to bring success. Reluctantly, for they were very close, his mother gave her consent. The expenses came to more than anyone had guessed; at last Kasturbai had to sell her jewelry to buy the ticket, and Gandhi's older brother gave his promise to pay the rest.

Gandhi had made a few previous trips by bullock cart to towns a few miles away. Like any eighteen-year-old, he expected the sea voyage to England to be full of excitement and adventure. Instead he found it haunted by loneliness. Shy and self-conscious, afraid to make himself look foolish with his schoolbook English, he kept to himself on board the ship and lingered for hours at the railings watching the sea. At mealtimes he stayed in his cabin and lived on sweets his mother had packed away. He had selected a white flannel suit to wear when he landed, but was agonized to find himself the only man in London dressed in white.

His first few months in England were a nightmare. Everything around him was different; everything he said or did was out of place. Manners, clothes, expressions, the meaning of the slightest gesture – all these had to be learned, often through error and ridicule. He could not shake off his homesickness. Never had he been so alone.

"I would continuously think of my home and country. My mother's love always haunted me. At night the tears would stream down my cheeks, and home memories of all sorts made sleep out of the question. It was impossible to share my misery with anyone. And even if I could have done so, where was the use? I knew of nothing that would soothe me. Everything was strange. . . ."

For weeks Gandhi was on the verge of turning back and taking the next boat home. But his pride would not allow it. Something deeper within him was determined to stick it out.

At last an Indian acquaintance who knew his way around London took pity on him. "You're not here to learn law," he scolded. "You're here to learn the English way of life. What are you doing holed up by yourself in this hotel?" Gandhi saw the point. The English had ruled his country for over two hundred years; to almost every Indian, no matter what his allegiance, they were the symbol of humanity's greatest achievements in civilization and physical power. Even by coming to England he was tacitly acknowledging their superiority. Meekly he followed his friend's advice and found a room with an English family.

It was Gandhi's first experiment in mimicking lifestyles. Whenever something appealed to him, even as a boy, his first impulse had always been to try it out for himself. Now he decided to become an English gentleman. He engaged tutors in French and proper speaking, and bought expensive tailored suits and a silk top hat. He taught himself how to tie a necktie, and learned to admire himself before a mirror while he struggled to discipline his hair with an English brush. He even invested in violin lessons and tried to learn the fox-trot.

But the role of the gentleman failed to meet his needs. Far from giving him greater security, it only made him more self-conscious, more acutely aware of what others might think of how he looked and acted. Moreover, it was an expensive way of life, and since his brother was supporting him, he felt uneasy about spending his money so lavishly. The gap he sensed between his inner and outward selves was widening into a chasm.

After about three months Gandhi awoke abruptly from these dreams of grandeur. How could changing the way he dressed make him anything more than what he already was? To change his life he had to change his way of thinking, and that was something that went deeper than any differences in custom or culture. Better to be truthful to oneself than to try to act like someone else. "If my character made a gentleman of me," he wrote, "so much the better. Otherwise I should forego the ambition." He began to experiment with a simpler way of life.

With members of the
Vegetarian Society,
London, 1890. Gandhi
is in the bottom row
at the right.
(Courtesy Sumati Morarjee
and Vithalbhai K. Jhaveri)

His first step was to find an apartment of his own. He gave up all lessons in social improvement, sold his violin, and began to concentrate on his studies. Then, when he discovered an impoverished student who lived in only one room and cooked his own meals, Gandhi immediately followed the example, selecting a room which was centrally located so that he could walk wherever he needed to go instead of taking the bus. It could have been a limitation; he turned it instead into an opportunity. His long walks kept him alert and strong even in the harsh London winter, and formed a habit which he kept up throughout his life. Most important, there was a self-reliance in these

18

experiments which he had missed in imitating others. He found himself not only healthier but happier for the change.

Then he began to experiment with his diet.

Gandhi's family was vegetarian, and before he left home he had promised his mother that he would not eat meat as the English did, though he was convinced it was one of the secrets of their strength. English friends and Indian students alike tried to persuade him that meat was essential for good health, especially in the colder climate of England. But Gandhi, though half afraid they were right, was determined not to break his promise. For months he found nothing to eat in the whole of London but bread and boiled spinach. Finally, driven by hunger, he began to investigate vegetarianism scientifically. He found a group of Englishmen who were zealous vegetarians and read their books on diet and health. Their ideas seemed well argued; Gandhi decided to put them to the test. He tried all sorts of vegetarian combinations to see which worked best for him and began giving up whatever seemed harmful, even if it was good to the taste. Gradually, deprived of the pungent spices of Indian cooking, he began to taste the food itself instead, and realized he was relishing dishes which had been a torture to eat before. He had discovered that the sense of taste lies not in the tongue but in the mind.

But Gandhi still had not found a real direction. Becoming a barrister proved no challenge; all he had to do was to pass some notoriously easy examinations and be present for a minimum number of dinners at the Inns of Court in London. He tried to learn law anyway, despite the irrelevance of his exams, but there was no motivation to connect what he read to anything he knew. Frustrated, he tried his hand at social reform through the Vegetarian Society in London, but his awkwardness still overwhelmed him. He could not express the simplest opinions even before a sympathetic committee. He was clumsy and tongue-tied in every social situation. He read all the required lawbooks diligently, but was continually torn by doubts and anxieties over his ability to plead a case in court.

After three years in London Gandhi passed his examinations, was called to the bar, and enrolled in High Court. The very next day he sailed for home. News of his mother's illness had distressed him deeply, and he was anxious to put London behind him and get home. But his own inadequacies overwhelmed him, and he was full of misgivings about his future.

His fears proved well founded. He arrived in Bombay harbor in the middle of a dreary tropical summer squall, and the wind and the rain outside, he wrote, only matched the storm of doubt within his heart. His older brother was waiting for him at the dock; their mother, he said, had died before Gandhi could return. Knowing how much he loved her, they had withheld the news.

Gandhi buried his grief and tried to turn his face toward the promise of his legal future. But in Rajkot, his high school town, he was an immediate failure. Not only did he not know how to apply legal principles to particular situations, his English book-learning left him without the slightest knowledge of Indian law. No one would dream of giving him a case.

In Bombay he fared no better. His colleagues began to refer to him laughingly as the "briefless barrister." With time on his hands he went to the High Court every day to gain experience. But the talk was dull and droned on endlessly; Gandhi had trouble following the cases and often dozed off in the middle of them. His first and only case in Bombay was a routine, ten-dollar claim. Gandhi stood up with trembling knees to make his cross-examination, but discovered abruptly that he could not utter a single word. Finally, amidst his colleagues' laughter, he handed the case over to someone with more experience and fled from the room.

It was at this point that Gandhi's life took one of those mysteriously fruitful turns that some observers like to ascribe to "fate" or "chance." Gandhi himself, looking back on his life from the vantage point of decades of inner evolution, called it instead an act of grace, the unfolding of events according to some deep inner necessity of which he himself was unaware. Battered by failure, with nowhere left to look for help outside, he was ready to turn inward on his long journey of self-discovery. Chance, or grace, provided him with the challenge.

At the time it did not seem like much of an opportunity. Through his brother, a local Muslim firm offered to help Gandhi out with a year's contract with its office in South Africa. It was a minor clerical position, well below the salary and prestige his English education deserved. And it meant more separation from Kasturbai, who had just borne them a second son. But Gandhi jumped at the opportunity. It was, at least, a job, a chance to gain some experience and maybe turn his back forever on his bad luck.

But the situation awaiting him was far from what he had expected. Dada Abdulla's Indian office had misunderstood his South African office's needs. The case Gandhi was called in on was a complicated one, requiring real skill in accounting to unravel years of complicated business transactions with inadequate records. Gandhi's job was to advise the company's legal counsel, but he was even more ignorant of bookkeeping than he was of law. Moreover, far from gaining any respect by his new move, he found himself in a land where the color of his skin alone was enough to mark him off for daily contempt and even physical abuse. He had taken all his problems with him with his luggage.

Gandhi was always a good observer of his own behavior. Every time that he had run away from failure before, no matter where he went, the same situation always seemed to recur in even more threatening proportions. This time he might have languished with pay in Dada Abdulla's offices attending to minor correspondence for twelve months and then gone home, no less a failure than before. Instead he decided to try a different attack. If changing his environment did no good, why not try to change himself? It was not something he reasoned out; it was something he felt so deeply that action was immediate. He took the challenge and threw himself into the work at hand.

Almost immediately the self-discipline he had learned in London began to pay off. He studied bookkeeping on his own and found with increasing self-confidence that his intellect proved equal to the need. Exhilarated, he strained every faculty of concentration in him to ferret out all the details of the case and find the truth. He acquired a deeper knowledge of the situation than anyone else on either side.

The facts were strongly behind his client. But the legal battle could be drawn out for months; no one stood to gain except the lawyers. Gandhi was not interested in making a profit out of legal briefs and empty arguments. He was determined to serve the best interests of both sides. Dada Abdulla and his opponent were blood relations, and every day the case dragged on only drove in deeper the wedge that was splitting their family in two. With much talking Gandhi persuaded both sides to submit to arbitration and settle out of court. Even more talking was necessary to get Dada Abdulla to agree on terms which would not bankrupt the loser, but in the end both sides were satisfied. Gandhi was ecstatic. "I had learnt," he exclaimed, "the true practice of law. I had learnt to find out the better side of human nature and to enter men's hearts. I realized that the true function of a lawyer was to unite parties riven asunder."

Without realizing it, Gandhi had found the secret of success. He began to look on every difficulty as an opportunity for service, a challenge which could draw out of him greater resources of intelligence and imagination. In turning his back on personal profit or prestige in his work, he found he had won the trust and even love of white and Indian South Africans alike. More and more people from his own community began to entrust their legal work to him and to depend on him whenever they needed help. In a few years he was a successful lawyer with an income of about twenty-five or thirty thousand dollars a year and a dignified, Westernized style of living appropriate to his station.

Satisfied for the time being, Gandhi returned to India to bring Kasturbai and their two sons back to their new home. Painfully they adjusted to the tortures of alien clothes and artificial manners. At first they objected bitterly, but Gandhi was unyielding. It was essential to look "civilized" – that is, European. That was the price of success, and all of them had to pay it. Kasturbai could not have been entirely dissatisfied. At twenty-seven, her husband was on the crest of the wave of fortune; everything they could want seemed at last within his grasp. He had reached the stage where most young men's experimentation comes to an end.

But the political and social repression of all Indians in South Africa, and especially the desperate condition of those who came as laborers on a system equivalent to legalized slavery, had made a deep impression on Gandhi. One of these men, who had been beaten

In London, 1906.

(UPI)

22

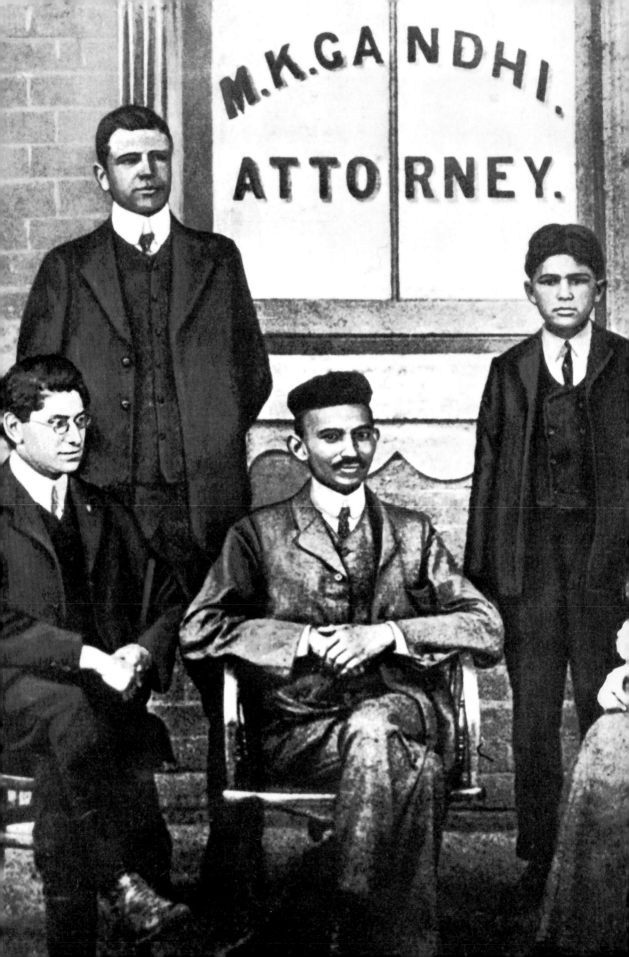

severely by his employer, came to Gandhi for help, and through him Gandhi got to know many others. He visited their homes, came to know their families and how they lived. Gradually he began to forget about himself in trying to find time and resources to alleviate the suffering of these people. They were his brothers and sisters; he identified with them more every day. Their suffering became his suffering.

When the black plague broke out in the squalid Indian ghetto of Johannesburg, the sick and dying were taken to an abandoned, quarantined building where a heroic English nurse spent long hours alone caring for them. Many years later she related that in the evening at the height of the epidemic a small figure appeared at the door. She shouted a warning: "Get out! This is plague." But the man quietly replied, "It's all right. I've come to help you."

She recognized him as a leader of the Indian community and let him in. He went straight to the sick. As she saw him bend over a dying man covered with vermin, she said, "Leave him; I'm used to it." But Gandhi attended the man himself and whispered back: "He is my brother." And he stayed throughout the night until relief came.

"My profession progressed satisfactorily, but that was far from satisfying me. The question of further simplifying my life and of doing some concrete act of service to my fellowmen had been constantly agitating me, when a leper came to my door. I had not the heart to dismiss him with a meal. So I offered him shelter, dressed his wounds, and began to look after him...."

Gandhi's law offices
in Johannesburg, 1905.
At the right is Sonya
Schlesin, one of his
most intimate
co-workers in South
Africa.
(Courtesy Sumati Morarjee
and Vithalbhai K. Jhaveri)

"I had started on a life of ease and comfort, but the experiment was short-lived. Although I had furnished the house with care, yet it failed to have any hold on me. So no sooner had I launched forth on that life, than I began to cut down expenses. The washerman's bill was heavy, and as he was besides by no means noted for his punctuality, even two to three dozen shirts and collars proved insufficient for me. Collars had to be changed daily and shirts, if not daily, at least every alternate day. This meant a double expense which appeared to me unnecessary. So I equipped myself with a washing outfit to save it. I bought a book on washing, studied the art and taught it also to my wife. This no doubt added to my work, but its novelty made it a pleasure.

"I shall never forget the first collar that I washed myself. I had used more starch than necessary, the iron had not been made hot enough, and for fear of burning the collar I had not pressed it sufficiently. The result was that, though the collar was fairly stiff, the superfluous starch continually dropped off it. I went to court with the collar on, thus inviting the ridicule of brother barristers, but even in those days I could be impervious to ridicule. . . .

"In the same way, as I freed myself from slavery to the washerman, I threw off dependence on the barber. All people who go to England learn there at least the art of shaving, but none, to my knowledge, learn to cut their own hair. I had to learn that too. I once went to an English haircutter in Pretoria. He contemptuously refused to cut my hair. I certainly felt hurt, but immediately purchased a pair of clippers and cut my hair before the mirror. I succeeded more or less in cutting the front hair, but I spoiled the back. The friends in the court shook with laughter.

"'What's wrong with your hair, Gandhi? Rats have been at it?'

"'No. The white barber would not condescend to touch my black hair,' said I, 'so I preferred to cut it myself, no matter how badly.'"

As a lawyer, South
Africa, 1906.

(Courtesy Maniam Natesan)

The ideal of selfless service had taken hold of Gandhi and caused rapid changes in every aspect of his life. The financial returns of a successful law career, the European style of living, the complicated household – all these fell away when they became obstacles in his path of community service. Each simplification freed time, energy, and ability. Often, especially at first, it was painful to give up his time or pleasure for the sake of others' needs. But the freedom that followed was exhilarating. Gandhi's joy knew no bounds. Everywhere he began to see the possibility to choose between living for himself alone or living for the sake of others. He made time for volunteer nursing in the midst of a busy legal practice, started a weekly news magazine called *Indian Opinion,* and recruited an Indian ambulance corps to serve with the British army when war broke out with the Boer colonies in 1899. It was an infectious example, and a little family community or ashram began to grow up around him in the country outside Durban where a handful of dedicated young men and women, both European and Indian, came to live with him and share his experiments in the art

With the Indian
Ambulance Corps
during the Boer War,
1899. Gandhi, thirty, is
in the center.

(Courtesy *Indian Opinion*)

28

of living. As his self-centeredness diminished, his spiritual awareness increased. He began to study the scriptures of all religions and test their teachings against his own experience.

"'Do not worry in the least about yourself, leave all worry to God,' – this appears to be the commandment in all religions.

"This need not frighten anyone. He who devotes himself to service with a clear conscience, will day by day grasp the necessity for it in greater measure, and will continually grow richer in faith. The path of service can hardly be trodden by one who is not prepared to renounce self-interest, and to recognize the conditions of his birth. Consciously or unconsciously, every one of us does render some service or other. If we cultivate the habit of doing this service deliberately, our desire for service will steadily grow stronger, and will make not only for our own happiness but that of the world at large."

"One who would serve will not waste a thought upon his own comforts, which he leaves to be attended to or neglected by his Master on high. He will not, therefore, encumber himself with everything that comes his way; he will take only what he strictly needs and leave the rest. He will be calm, free from anger and unruffled in mind even if he finds himself inconvenienced. His service, like virtue, is its own reward, and he will rest content with it."

"Just as one must not receive, so must one not possess anything which one does not really need. It would be a breach of this principle to possess unnecessary foodstuffs, clothing, or furniture. For instance, one must not keep a chair if one can do without it. In observing this principle one is led to a progressive simplification of one's own life."

Gandhi was no longer to be seen in expensive European clothes. He had simplified every detail of his household. Kasturbai, after she had learned to eat with knife and fork and given over her household to her husband's infatuation for Western ways, had to unlearn all these things and go back to her original style of living. Then, for the sake of his convictions about social equality and the dignity of hard work, he made her tend the latrines of her own house – work that had always been done by the lowest castes of Indian society. She accepted out of love, though not without bitter protest. Gandhi later said her endurance was matchless.

But family life was still far from smooth. Once the Indians in Natal showered Gandhi with gifts. They had meant to express their appreciation for his work, but they only made Gandhi spend a sleepless night pacing the floor. He had taught his wife and sons that selfless service was its own reward. How could he now accept things given to him for service to his own community, work he had done without desire for personal profit? The gifts were valuable, of gold and silver, and there was a diamond necklace for his wife. They would be difficult to give up, but more difficult to keep. Near morning Gandhi sat down and drafted a letter creating a trust of the gifts to be used for community service.

Yet how was he to persuade Kasturbai to give up the jewels? She was adamant; they were the first such compensation they had received for several years of selfless work in which she had borne at least as many difficulties as he. She pleaded with him long and bitterly, and at last broke down in tears. Finally, more exhausted than persuaded, she consented to his demands. "I have never since regretted the step," wrote Gandhi, "and as the years have gone by my wife has also seen its wisdom. It has saved us from many temptations."

With Kasturbai, 1913.

(Courtesy Mathuradas

Trikamji)

"One man cannot do right in one department of life whilst he is occupied in doing wrong in any other department. Life is one indivisible whole."

The domestic struggles in South Africa were the training ground where Gandhi learned the demanding art of living for others rather than himself. Later he would apply the same lessons on a global scale, so that in the end the whole world became his family.

Many years later, long after he had left South Africa, Gandhi received a letter urging world leaders to draw up a charter of human rights. "In my experience," Gandhi wrote back, "it is far more important to have a charter of human duties."

It was an approach he had learned from Kasturbai. When he came back from his student years in London, Gandhi explained, fully cultured and acutely conscious of his "legitimate rights," the first person he tried to impress with all this status was his wife. Kasturbai Gandhi, however, was a woman with a will of her own. Gandhi began to demand his rights the minute he came home; and Kasturbai, naturally, started to do the same – at the same time, in the same house. Often their disagreements became so fierce that Kasturbai was reduced to tears, which only irritated Gandhi more. Once, exasperated, he shouted at her: "I will not stand this nonsense in my house!"

"Then keep your house to yourself," Kasturbai pleaded, "and let me go!"

In a rage Gandhi grabbed her by the arm and dragged her weeping to the gate.

"Have you no sense of shame?" she cried through her tears. "Where can I go? I have no family here to take me in. Because I am your wife, do you think I have to put up with your abuse? For heaven's sake behave yourself and shut the gate. Let's not be caught making such a scene!"

It is Gandhi himself who relates the incident. At the time, he says, he thought it was his right as a husband to impose his opinions on his wife. But as the years passed and the storms between them continued, he began to realize what anguish he was causing her by this rigid outlook. At last it occurred to him that rather than exercise his "rights," he could fulfill his responsibilities. With Gandhi, to know was to feel, to feel was to act, to act was to live. Immediately, instead of forcing Kasturbai's obedience to his newfound beliefs and values, he began to try to win her over by his own example. It was a long, painful process,

Kasturbai in 1915.

(Courtesy Maniam Natesan)

33

and often Gandhi had to ignore his cherished likes and dislikes to see things from her point of view rather than his own. But gradually he began to see that there was no friction between them except what he had imposed, and that Kasturbai had always been trying to win him over by love. It was one of the most radical discoveries he was to make in a lifetime of experimentation: in order to transform others, you first have to transform yourself.

Gandhi's experiments were leading him into rarely traveled regions deep below the surface level of living, where the ordinary values of buying and selling, prestige and pleasure, held no meaning at all. Writers and philosophers before him had written thick volumes on truth and happiness, but few of them had been able to change their lives. Gandhi was not interested in such abstract principles. He wanted to know how to live, and was willing to transform his whole personality, if necessary, to bring him closer to that goal. He scrutinized the lives and works of men from many other nationalities and faiths, looking for a guide. When he found one at last it was in the spiritual tradition of his own land, a tradition unbroken for more than five thousand years.

The Bhagavad Gita had always been near him while he was a child. Ironically, he did not begin to glimpse its practicality until he was in England: with English friends, reading an English translation. The first time he read it, he recalled, its words went straight to his heart. In South Africa they began to penetrate his actions as well. There the Gita became what he called his "spiritual reference book," the practical guide through the dangers and challenges he encountered as he deepened his search for truth.

In London, 1909.

(Courtesy Sumati Morarjee

and Vithalbhai K. Jhaveri)

35

"What effect this reading of the Gita had on my friends, only they can say; but to me the Gita became an infallible guide of conduct. It became my dictionary of daily reference. Just as I turned to the English dictionary for the meanings of English words that I did not understand, I turned to this dictionary of conduct for a ready solution of all my troubles and trials. Words like 'aparigraha' (non-possession) and 'samabhava' (equability) gripped me. How to cultivate and preserve that equability was the question. How was one to treat alike insulting, insolent and corrupt officials, co-workers of yesterday raising meaning-less opposition, and men who had always been good to one? How was one to divest oneself of all possessions? . . . Was I to give up all I had and follow Him? Straight came the answer: I could not follow Him unless I gave up all I had.

"My study of English law came to my help. . . . I understood the Gita teaching of non-possession to mean that those who desired salvation should act like the trustee who, though having control over great possessions, regards not an iota of them as his own."

The Gita gives detailed instructions for crossing the sea of life. The battlefield where the narrative is set represents the individual human heart, where the forces of light and darkness, love and separateness, war incessantly for mastery over our thought and actions. In the dialogue which unfolds, Arjuna, the warrior prince who represents every man or woman, seeks to learn the art of living from Sri Krishna, the Lord of Love, who is the outward manifestation of Arjuna's deepest self. Arjuna is a man of action. He is not interested in metaphysics or airy theories; he wants to know how to make every moment of his life count, free from anxiety and fear. His questions are practical inquiries into the problems of living, and Sri Krishna's answers are simple and to the point. We are born to fight, he tells Arjuna; there is no choice in the matter. Our every desire must bring us into conflict. But we can choose how and whom we will fight. We can turn our anger against others, or we can turn it against what is selfish and angry in ourselves. We can use our hands to strike at others or to wipe their tears away. It is a call to action, and that is why Sri Krishna

With Kasturbai after their return to India from South Africa.

(The Bettmann Archive)

36

describes the heroes and heroines of the Gita's "way of love" in the language not of sentiment but of war:

All those I love who are incapable
Of ill will, and return love for hatred.
Living beyond the reach of *I* and *mine,*
And of pain and pleasure, full of mercy,
Contented, self-controlled, of firm resolve,
With all their heart and all their mind given
To Me – with such as these I am in love.

Not agitating the world, nor by it
Agitated, they stand above the sway
Of elation, competition and fear,
Accepting life, good and bad, as it comes.
They are pure, efficient, detached, ready
To meet every demand I make on them
As a humble instrument of My work....

Who serves both friend and foe with equal love,
Not buoyed up by praise nor cast down by blame,
Alike in heat and cold, pleasure and pain,
Free from selfish attachments and self-will,
Ever full, in harmony everywhere,
Firm in faith – such a one is dear to Me.

It was in South Africa that Gandhi learned to translate these tremendous ideals into effective action. Inspired by the response to his nursing efforts during the Boer War, he had recruited a second Indian ambulance corps to help the Natal government put down a "rebellion" among the Zulu natives. This time, however, he found no glory on the field. The "rebellion" turned out to be just an excuse for a manhunt which opened Gandhi's eyes to the horrors of war. Every morning he woke up to the sound of gunshots as the British armies swept through and destroyed another Zulu village, and he and his volunteers had to march sometimes as much as forty miles a day with the bodies of innocent natives who had been mercilessly mistreated by the vengeful British soldiers. The senselessness of their suffering would not let him rest. Night and day, carrying their stretchers across the vast deserted hill country of Natal, he plunged himself deep into prayer and self-examination in a fervent search for greater strength with which to serve.

The intensity of his desire led him to the source of power itself. Deep in meditation Gandhi began to see how much of his vital energy was locked up in the sexual drive. In a flood of insight he realized that sex is not just a physical instinct, but an expression of the tremendous spiritual force behind all love and creativity which the Hindu scriptures call *kundalini*, the life-force of evolution. All his life it had been his master, buffeting him this way and that beyond his control. But in the silence of the Natal hills, with all his burning desire to serve focused by weeks of tending to the wounded and dying, Gandhi found the strength to tap this power at its source. Then and there he resolved to be its master and never to let it dictate to him again. It was a decision which resolved his deepest tensions and released all the love within him into his conscious control. He had begun to transform the last of his passions into spiritual power.

The Way of Love

The moment of decision had come for Gandhi in his first year in South Africa, when the work for Dada Abdulla took him inland across the state of Natal by railway and coach. European settlers in South Africa always traveled first class. Indians were expected to travel third, but Dada Abdulla had reserved a first-class seat for Gandhi. He settled into the compartment comfortably and traveled alone until he reached the high mountain town of Maritzburg in the evening. There another passenger, a European, entered the compartment. He took one look at the dark-complexioned man seated there and left, only to return with railway officials. "You'll have to leave here," one of them told Gandhi pointedly. "Go to the third-class car."

"But I have a ticket for this compartment," Gandhi objected.

"That doesn't matter. You must leave or I'll bring the police to put you out."

"You may," Gandhi agreed heatedly. "But I have every right to stay here, and I refuse to get out voluntarily."

So the policeman came and Gandhi was pushed out of the train and left to spend the night sitting in the deserted, unlit railway station of Maritzburg. His overcoat and luggage had disappeared with the officials. It was bitter cold. He sat there alone, shivering in the darkness, struggling furiously to understand how anyone could find pleasure or satisfaction in causing suffering to others. It was not his own injury or humiliation that infuriated him; it was the much deeper cancer of man's inhumanity to man, the persecution of whole races because of differences in skin color or belief.

By morning he had decided that to return to India would be cowardice. He would have to stay; there could be no turning back. He was compelled to act. The man who had been unable to talk in court to

As a lawyer in Johannesburg, 1900.

(Courtesy Sumati Morarjee and Vithalbhai K. Jhaveri)

enhance his own career would find within himself the resources to speak and write and organize effectively to relieve the distress of others.

Much later, when someone asked him what was the most creative incident in his life, Gandhi told the story of this night in Maritzburg station. He had to undergo many trials, suffer abuse and even physical attacks, but that long night in the Natal mountains he made the decision never to yield to force and never to use force to win a cause.

42

"I object to violence because when it appears to do good, the good is only temporary; the evil it does is permanent."

"I do not believe in short-violent-cuts to success.... However much I may sympathize with and admire worthy motives, I am an uncompromising opponent of violent methods even to serve the noblest of causes.... Experience convinces me that permanent good can never be the outcome of untruth and violence."

But it was not until thirteen years later, when Gandhi was thirty-seven, that this deep conviction blossomed into the inspiration for mass nonviolent resistance. Gandhi had just returned from his ambulance duty during the Zulu "rebellion," fresh from his decision to devote his life completely to community service. The opportunity was waiting. The white government of the Transvaal had introduced new legislation to deprive South African Indians of what civil rights they still retained under the law. If the "Black Act" were passed it would mean the end of the Indian communities in South Africa. A great crowd of Indians gathered in Johannesburg at Gandhi's suggestion to decide on a course of resistance. Gandhi had not come prepared with any plan; he only knew that it was "better to die than to submit to such a law." But in the midst of that passionate crowd, ready for any extreme of violence, the inspiration came to him to offer an even higher challenge: to refuse to obey such degrading legislation and accept the consequences without violent retaliation but without yielding an inch in their demand for fair and equal treatment under the law. Every man and woman present rose to meet the challenge and pledged nonviolent resistance even to the point of death. "Thus came into being," Gandhi wrote triumphantly, "the moral equivalent of war."

"Civil disobedience is the inherent right of a citizen. He dare not give it up without ceasing to be a man. Civil disobedience is never followed by anarchy. Criminal disobedience can lead to it. Every state puts down criminal disobedience by force. It perishes, if it does not. But to put down civil disobedience is to attempt to imprison conscience."

43

"Disobedience to be civil must be sincere, respectful, restrained, never defiant, must be based upon some well-understood principle, must not be capricious and, above all, must have no ill will or hatred behind it."

45

The movement spread swiftly through South Africa. What Gandhi proposed was an entirely new method of fighting. Instead of fanning hatred with hatred, violence with violence, he argued that exploitation could be overcome simply by returning love for hatred and respect for contempt, in a strong, determined refusal to yield to injustice. It was a style of resistance which demanded the highest courage, and such depth of commitment that every temporary setback only strengthened the resisters' determination more. Thousands of men, women, and children courted jail sentences in open but disciplined defiance of South African exploitation.

One of the first developments in Gandhi's campaign brought him straight to the head of the Transvaal government, General Jan Smuts. Gandhi had already developed the essentials of his later style, and it is easy to picture him sitting before this able Boer soldier and informing him quietly: "I've come to tell you that I am going to fight against your government."

Smuts must have thought he was hearing things. "You mean you have come here to tell me that?" he laughs. "Is there anything more you want to say?"

"Yes," says Gandhi. "I am going to win."

Smuts is astonished. "Well," he says at last, "and how are you going to do that?"

Gandhi smiles. "With your help."

Many years later Smuts admitted – not without humor – that this is exactly what Gandhi did. By his courage, by his determination, by his refusal to take unfair advantage, but especially by his endless capacity to "stick it out" without yielding and without retaliation, Gandhi managed at last to win the general's respect and friendship, and in 1914 the laws most offensive to the Indians were repealed and basic civil rights voted into law.

"Truth resides in every human heart, and one has to search for it there, and to be guided by truth as one sees it. But no one has a right to coerce others to act according to his own view of truth."

Satyagraha, the name Gandhi gave to this new way of overcoming injustice, means "holding on to truth" or "soul-force." *Satya* means "truth" in Sanskrit, and comes from *sat,* which means simply "that which is." The idea behind *satya* is that truth alone exists; for truth is not what holds good just at a certain time and place or under certain conditions, but that which never changes. Evil, injustice, hatred,

Gandhi argued, exist only insofar as we support them; they have no existence of their own. Without our cooperation, unintentional or intentional, injustice cannot continue.

This is the great spiritual teaching behind nonviolent noncooperation. As long as a people accepts exploitation, both exploiter and exploited will be entangled in injustice. But once the exploited refuse to accept the relationship, refuse to cooperate with it, they are already free.

Gandhi tested satyagraha in South Africa for seven years and showed that it worked even in a foreign land against a strong and hostile government. He returned to India a seasoned veteran of nonviolent resistance, certain that he could free India politically from British domination without war, without violence, if the Indian people would accept his leadership and abide completely by the nonviolent conditions he placed before them.

"Select your purpose," he challenged, "selfless, without any thought of personal pleasure or personal profit, and then use selfless means to attain your goal. Do not resort to violence even if it seems at first to promise success; it can only contradict your purpose. Use the means of love and respect even if the result seems far off or uncertain. Then throw yourself heart and soul into the campaign, counting no price too high for working for the welfare of those around you, and every reverse, every defeat, will send you deeper into your own deepest resources. Violence can never bring an end to violence; all it can do is provoke more violence. But if we can adhere to complete nonviolence in thought, word, and deed, India's freedom is assured."

With Herman Kallen-bach, one of his closest followers, in the Maritzburg train station during a satyagraha campaign, where years before he had made the silent vow never to yield to force and never to use force to win a cause.

(Courtesy *Indian Opinion*)

The historian J. B. Kripalani, who became one of Gandhi's closest co-workers, has said that the first time he heard Gandhi talk this way he was so shocked that he went up to him and told him point-blank: "Mr. Gandhi, you may know all about the Bible or the Bhagavad Gita, but you know nothing at all about history. Never has a nation been able to free itself without violence."

Gandhi smiled. "*You* know nothing about history," he corrected gently. "The first thing you have to learn about history is that because something has not taken place in the past, that does not mean it cannot take place in the future."

"In this age of wonders no one will say that a thing or an idea is worthless because it is new. To say it is impossible because it is difficult, is again not in consonance with the spirit of the age. Things undreamt of are daily being seen, the impossible is ever becoming possible. We are constantly being astonished these days at the amazing discoveries in the field of violence. But I maintain that far more undreamt of and seemingly impossible discoveries will be made in the field of nonviolence."

With the poet Sarojini Naidu, one of his most devoted associates, at the head of the Salt March, 1930. After Gandhi's "midnight arrest" on May 4, 1930, Sarojini Naidu, as Gandhi's second-in-command, led twenty-five hundred satya-grahis against some of the fiercest attacks in the struggle for inde-pendence.

(Courtesy Sumati Morarjee and Vithalbhai K. Jhaveri)

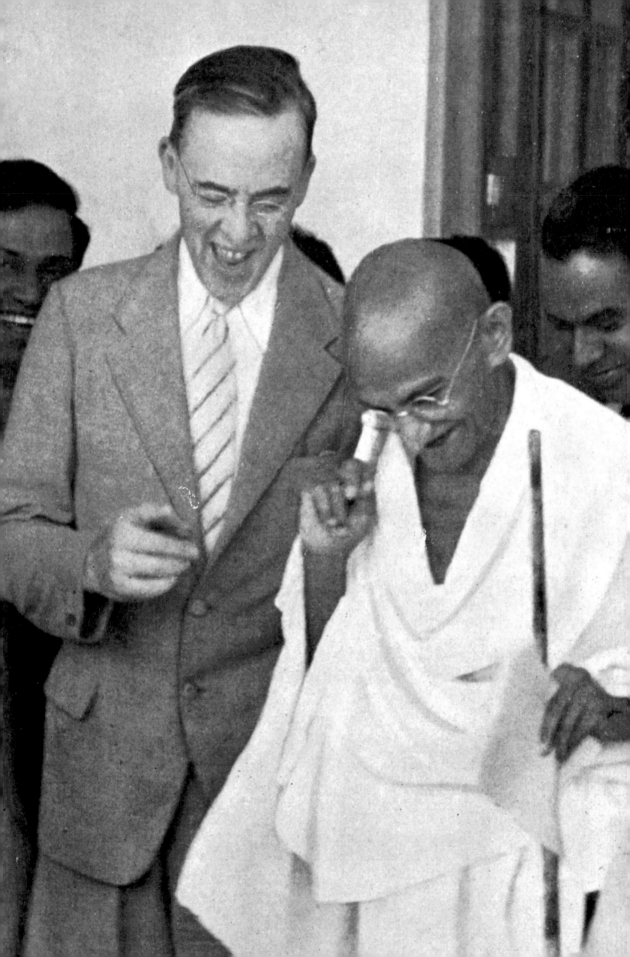

Satya and *ahimsa*, truth and nonviolence, became Gandhi's constant watchwords. In his experience they were "two sides of the same coin," two ways of looking at the same experiential fact. For him *satya* meant the deepest truth of existence, that all life is one. The proof was offered by the Compassionate Buddha: When one person hates another, it is the hater who falls ill – physically, emotionally, spiritually. When he loves, it is he who becomes whole. Hatred kills. Love heals.

Satyagraha means "holding to this truth" in every situation, no matter how fierce the storm. Because he wants nothing for himself, the true satyagrahi is not afraid of entering any conflict for the sake of those around him, without hostility, without resentment, without resorting even to violent words. Even in the face of the fiercest provocation, he never lets himself forget that he and his attacker are one. This is ahimsa, which is more than just the absence of violence; it is intense love.

The Sanskrit word *ahimsa* does not contain a negative or passive connotation as does the English translation "nonviolence." The implication of *ahimsa* is that when all violence subsides in the human heart, the state which remains is love. It is not something we have to acquire; it is always present, and needs only to be uncovered. This is our real nature, not merely to love one person here, another there, but to be love itself. Satyagraha is love in action.

"A satyagrahi bids goodbye to fear. He is therefore never afraid of trusting the opponent. Even if the opponent plays him false twenty times, the satyagrahi is ready to trust him the twenty-first time, for an implicit trust in human nature is the very essence of his creed."

"In satyagraha, it is never the numbers that count; it is always the quality, more so when the forces of violence are uppermost.

"Then it is often forgotten that it is never the intention of a satyagrahi to embarrass the wrongdoer. The appeal is never to his fear; it is, must be, always to his heart. The satyagrahi's object is to convert, not to coerce, the wrongdoer. He should avoid artificiality in all his doings. He acts naturally and from inward conviction."

"Satyagraha is gentle, it never wounds. It must not be the result of anger or malice. It is never fussy, never impatient, never vociferous. It is the direct opposite of compulsion. It was conceived as a complete substitute for violence."

With the British

governor of Bengal in

1945. Gandhi is

observing a day of

silence and answering

by means of notes.

(UPI)

Ahimsa is our *dharma*, the central law of our being, written into our every cell. The "law of the jungle," Gandhi used to say, is all right for animals; violence is their dharma. But for men and women to be violent is to reverse the course of evolution and go against their deepest nature, which is to love, to endure, to forgive.

"I hold myself to be incapable of hating any being on earth. By a long course of prayerful discipline, I have ceased for over forty years to hate anybody. I know this is a big claim. Nevertheless, I make it in all humility.

"But I can and do hate evil wherever it exists. I hate the system of government that the British people have set up in India. I hate the ruthless exploitation of India even as I hate from the bottom of my heart the hideous system of untouchability for which millions of Hindus have made themselves responsible. But I do not hate the domineering Englishmen as I refuse to hate the domineering Hindus. I seek to reform them in all the loving ways that are open to me. My noncooperation has its roots not in hatred, but in love."

For centuries, millions of people in India had been subjected to great cruelty and discrimination by the higher classes in the name of the caste system. Gandhi, having learned from personal experience the great truth "As ye sow, so shall ye reap," saw a deep underlying connection between India's exploitation of these impoverished millions and Great Britain's exploitation of the Indian people. One of the first steps he took to restore India's self-respect and unity was to begin the liberation of these lower classes. The former name for these people – a terrible one in Sanskrit – means "those who cannot be touched." The name itself perpetuated their sense of inferiority and shame. But Gandhi began to change this status overnight by giving them a different title: Harijans, the children of God.

He campaigned from the Himalayas south to Ceylon. Everywhere the message was the same: "All of us are one. When you inflict suffering on others, you are bringing suffering on yourself. When you weaken others, you are weakening yourself, weakening the whole nation." On some occasions he would shame all India by refusing to

At a prayer meeting in a small village in Noakhali during Hindu-Muslim riots, 1946.

(Courtesy Tarak Das)

enter the great temples whose gates had been closed for centuries to low-caste Hindu worshippers. "There is no God here," he would tell the crowds who gathered to hear him. "If God were here, everyone would have access. He is in every one of us." Because of the love the people bore him, such words went in very deep. Temples and homes throughout India, after centuries of exclusion, began to open their doors to all.

Wherever Gandhi went he collected money for the Harijans. Many Indian women, particularly in the villages, used to wear every gold ornament they owned, and there was a saying that a man's best bank is his wife's neck. Gandhi found this a little ostentatious when so much of the country was near starvation, and he took every opportunity to appeal to such women to give up their gold necklaces, earrings, and bangles to be sold for Harijan service. Not even children were safe from this prince of beggars. He was so irresistible that whenever his train pulled into a station, no matter what time of the day or night, great crowds of people of all ages would be waiting to press their money and jewelry into his outstretched hands.

Trains in India have three classes. In those days, first-class accommodations were meant only for the ruling classes – the British – while the second class was taken by the upper strata of Indian society. The third class – crowded, dirty wooden benches – was left for the vast majority of Indians, the poor. Gandhi, who dramatized his unity with the poor by sharing their way of life completely, always preferred to travel third class on these campaigns. When someone asked him why, he answered simply: "Because there is no fourth."

On one occasion during these campaigns an obviously well-off missionary came to Gandhi to get his advice on how to help the outcaste people of the Indian villages. Gandhi's answer challenged the very basis of his life: "We must step down from our pedestals and live with them – not as outsiders, but as one of them in every way, sharing their burdens and sorrows."

Collecting for the

Harijan fund from a

third-class railway car.

(Courtesy Sarvodaya Diwas

Samiti)

This is the heart of Gandhi's approach. He taught, above all, by personal example. He went and lived with the Harijans; and to encourage them to improve their health and sanitation, he himself became their servant. Hundreds of his followers made their homes in poor villages throughout India, living with the people, teaching and encouraging them by their own example to release themselves from the bondage of ignorance, squalor, superstition, and the utter poverty which followed three hundred years of foreign exploitation. Gandhi once wrote to one of these workers, an Englishwoman named Mary Barr, that if the suffering of the poor masses of India could be alleviated without removing the British mountain from Indian soil, he would not fight for India's independence but would remain loyal to the empire. But it was the poor who suffered most from British domination, and so it was for their sake that he was drawn at last into the struggle for Indian freedom.

"To see the universal and all-pervading Spirit of Truth face to face one must be able to love the meanest of creation as oneself. And a man who aspires after that cannot afford to keep out of any field of life. That is why my devotion to Truth has drawn me into the field of politics; and I can say without the slightest hesitation, and yet in all humility, that those who say that religion has nothing to do with politics do not know what religion means."

In the early stages of India's struggle for independence there were many harsh incidents which deface the pages of British history. When Gandhi returned from South Africa, during the First World War, India was seething with the threat of violent revolution under the repressive cover of martial law. At last satyagraha seemed to be the only remedy for the brutality of colonial misrule, and prisons began to fill as thousands of men and women responded to Gandhi's challenge to cease all cooperation with the institutions of British government. Punishment was swift, and jail terms severe. But each arrest only seemed to inspire others to give up their government jobs, stop paying taxes, and court imprisonment themselves.

Finally Gandhi too was arrested, on the charge of inciting sedition. His trial – the only one the government ever granted him – gave him a forum for a detailed, scathing indictment of British exploitation. India and the rest of the world began to see that it was not Gandhi, but imperialism itself which was on trial.

In Bihar, 1934.

(Courtesy Dr. Rajendra

Prasad)

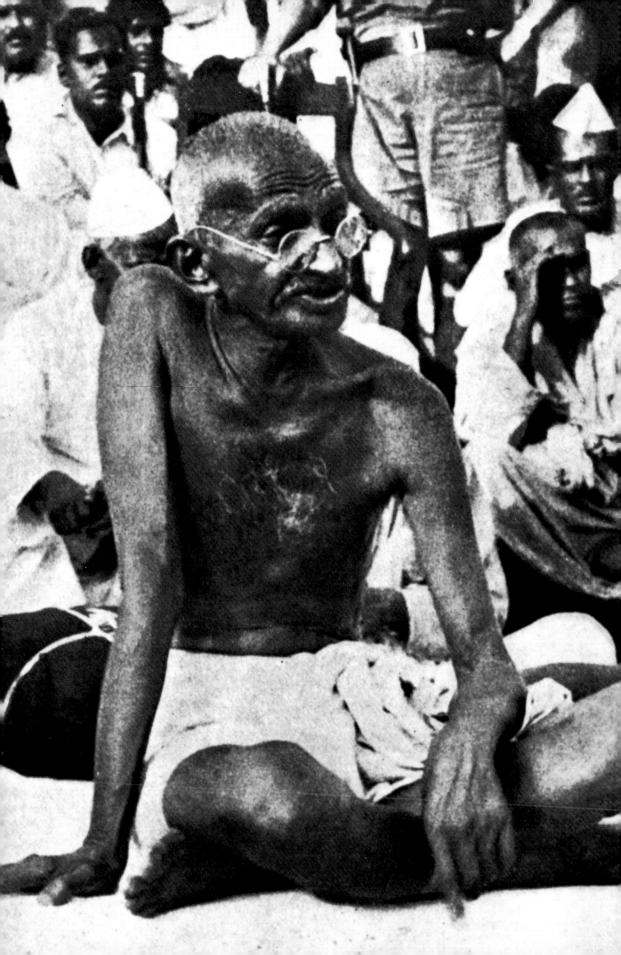

"I have no desire whatsoever to conceal from this court the fact that to preach disaffection toward the existing system of Government has become almost a passion with me. . . ."

"Little do town dwellers know how the semi-starved masses of India are slowly sinking to lifelessness. Little do they know that their miserable comfort represents the brokerage they get for their work they do for the foreign exploiter, that the profits and the brokerage are sucked from the masses. Little do they realize that the Government established by law in British India is carried on for this exploitation of the masses. No sophistry, no jugglery in figures, can explain away the evidence that the skeletons in many villages present to the naked eye."

"I believe that I have rendered a service to India and England by showing in noncooperation the way out of the unnatural state in which both are living. In my opinion, noncooperation with evil is as much a duty as is cooperation with good. But in the past, noncooperation has been deliberately expressed in violence to the evil-doer. I am endeavoring to show to my countrymen that violent noncooperation only multiplies evil, and that as evil can only be sustained by violence, withdrawal of support of evil requires complete abstention from violence.

"Nonviolence implies voluntary submission to the penalty for noncooperation with evil. I am here, therefore, to invite and submit cheerfully to the highest penalty that can be inflicted upon me for what in law is deliberate crime, and what appears to me to be the highest duty of a citizen. The only course open to you, the judge and the assessors, is either to resign your posts and thus dissociate yourselves from evil, if you feel that the law you are called upon to administer is an evil, and that in reality I am innocent, or to inflict on me the severest penalty, if you believe that the system and the law you are assisting to administer are good for the people of this country, and that my activity is, therefore, injurious to the common weal."

In 1931.

(Courtesy N. J. Nalawala)

It was in these early years of noncooperation that Gandhi attracted some of his closest friends and co-workers, men and women from very different backgrounds and nationalities who shared one central experience: each had come to Gandhi to observe and stayed to serve. Just to meet him was to run the risk of being turned into a hero, and the lives of countless numbers of ordinary men, women, and even children were transformed completely by this one little man, who demanded – and got – from everyone the highest order of selflessness and love. Even his enemies were not immune. "Don't go near Gandhi," new British administrators were warned when they went to assume their duties in India. "Don't go near Gandhi; he'll get you."

Jawaharlal Nehru was one of the first in India to suffer this fate. His father, Motilal Nehru, was a powerful lawyer from a very cultured and wealthy Hindu family. When young Jawaharlal returned to India from Cambridge, used to playing cricket and skiing in the Alps, he was a complete stranger to his own land and people. But though at home with British customs he still chafed under British rule, and fell in immediately with the passionate young revolutionaries for whom nonviolent noncooperation seemed too slow a road to freedom.

Gandhi disarmed him completely. "You people are always talking about revolution," he told them. "I am making one. What is revolutionary about violence? If you really love your people, help me show them how to turn their backs on violence and throw off their fear."

The challenge went straight to Nehru's heart. It did not matter that he and Gandhi were poles apart in many of their attitudes and beliefs; the man himself was too magnificent to resist. Nehru gave up his fine clothes and expensive habits and began to pour all his wealth and talent into Gandhi's movement for independence.

It was too much for his father. Motilal Nehru had given Jawaharlal the best upbringing that money could buy, and because he loved his son deeply it must have hurt him a great deal to see all these things apparently thrown away. At last he went to Gandhi for a private confrontation. "You have taken our only son," he pleaded. "Give him back to us, and I will put my wealth at the disposal of your campaigns."

Gandhi listened to him patiently, but only shook his head. "Not only do I want your son," he said with a mischievous smile, "I want you, and your wife, and your daughters, and the rest of your family too." And he got them, one by one, beginning with Motilal himself.

Gandhi was the most bewildering opponent any nation ever faced. Every move he made was spontaneous; every year that passed found him more youthful, more radical, more experimental. British administrators were baffled and exasperated by this little man who with-

drew when they would have attacked, attacked when they would have withdrawn, and seemed to be getting stronger day by day. No one knew what he was going to do next, for his actions were prompted not by calculations of what seemed politically expedient, but by a deep intuition which often came to him only in the eleventh hour.

Never was this more evident than in the Salt Satyagraha of 1930, which brought Gandhi and the Indian struggle to the attention of the world. Up until that time, for the sake of compromise, India had been seeking only dominion status within the British Empire. But ten years of bitter repression had passed since the era of noncooperation

With Jawaharlal Nehru.

(Courtesy- Press Information Bureau)

65

began, and Great Britain had only tightened its hold on the Indian people. On the first of January, 1930, at the stroke of midnight, the Indian Congress party raised the flag of a new nation to usher in the struggle for complete independence.

Everyone looked to Gandhi to see what would happen next. A new satyagraha campaign seemed imminent, but no one, including Gandhi, had any idea of what it would be or when it would be launched. Weeks passed. The threat of violence mounted higher, but Gandhi remained silent. The government waited anxiously, afraid to arrest him, afraid to leave him free.

Finally, after weeks of deliberation, the answer came to Gandhi in a dream. It was breathtakingly simple. The government had imposed a law forbidding Indians to make their own salt, making them dependent on a British monopoly for what is, in a tropical country, a necessity of life. To Gandhi it was the perfect symbol of colonial exploitation. He proposed to march with seventy-eight of his most trusted ashram followers to the little coastal town of Dandi, some two hundred forty miles away, where salt from the sea lay free for the taking on the sand. When he gave the signal, everyone in India was to act as if the salt laws had never been enacted at all.

When the scheduled morning arrived an immense crowd gathered outside Gandhi's ashram to catch what might be a final glimpse of this little figure who was about to turn all India upside down. It was an epic march, with the attention of news audiences everywhere riveted on every stage of the way. Gandhi was sixty-one, but he had never been in better shape. He marched with the light, brisk step of an athlete, covering about twelve miles a day, stopping at every village on the way to preach the gospel of ahimsa and the duty of nonviolent noncooperation. Everywhere he passed people streamed out to meet him, lining the roads between towns and strewing his path with flowers. By the time he reached Dandi, twenty-four days later, his nonviolent army of seventy-eight had swelled to several thousand.

Throughout the night of their arrival Gandhi and his followers prayed for the strength to resist the violence which might easily sweep away so large a crowd. Then, at the moment of dawn, they went quietly down to the water, and Gandhi, with thousands of eyes

watching every gesture, stooped down and picked up a pinch of salt from the sand.

The response was immediate. All along India's coastline huge crowds of men, women, and children swept down to the sea to gather salt in direct disobedience of the British laws. Their contraband salt was auctioned off at premium prices to those in the cities who could break the law only by buying. The whole country knew it had thrown off its chains, and despite the brutality of the police reprisals, the atmosphere was one of nationwide rejoicing. Months later, while negotiating at teatime with Lord Irwin, Gandhi took a little paper bag out of the folds of his cloak and, before the viceroy's astonished eyes, dropped a little of its contents into his cup. "I will put a little of this salt into my tea," he explained mischievously, "to remind us of the famous Boston Tea Party." Lord Irwin had the grace to join in his laughter.

Civil disobedience erupted spontaneously throughout the country for weeks after Gandhi's signal. Thousands were arrested; many more were beaten or killed without a hint of violent retaliation. Unaccountably, Gandhi remained free. He alone maintained order in that vast, unpredictable movement which was shaking the Indian subcontinent from the Himalayas to the sea.

One night following another massive arrest a crowd had gathered for the evening prayer meeting at Gandhi's work camp, a few small open huts of palm and date leaves halfway between Dandi and the sea. That night Gandhi's talk was more serious than usual, and after the prayers and singing a long list of those arrested was read aloud by the fading light of a hurricane lamp. Usually the crowds broke up after these meetings, and Gandhi and his co-workers retired for the night. But this evening few could sleep. Gandhi's arrest seemed imminent, and everyone was full of suspense and speculation, anxious for his welfare.

The police officials arrived at midnight, accompanied by thirty men with readied guns. In the darkness it was impossible for them to make out Gandhi anywhere, or guess where he might be hiding.

At last someone pointed out a little white bundle in one of the open sheds. "That is Gandhiji." In the midst of the confusion the

PREVIOUS

SPREAD:

Leaving Ahmedabad

on the morning of

March 12, 1930, the

first day of the Salt

March.

(Lt.-Col. B. J. Bhatt, Ret.)

leader of this national earthquake was sleeping like a baby, absolutely certain that the Lord would take care of him.

The British official awakened the sleeper and shone a flashlight into his face. "We have come to arrest Mr. M. K. Gandhi."

"I am Mohandas Karamchand Gandhi," the little figure answered politely. "I am at your service."

"Please get your things ready. We will give you the time you need."

"I am ready now," said Gandhi, indicating the small bundle on the floor. "This is all I need."

While the policemen watched he set about brushing his few teeth in his usual unhurried way. Then after a short prayer he turned to the official in charge and walked briskly to the car outside, chatting cheerfully to his escorts. He knew that it might be years before he returned, yet there was no trace of apprehension or resentment in his manner. The police were so impressed by the simple dignity of this little man that they seemed to be not his jailers but his prisoners. He was at his very best when being persecuted. He was at his strongest when under pressure. And he was free whether inside prison or out.

At work in Sevagram

ashram.

(Courtesy Kanu Gandhi)

By this time over sixty thousand satyagrahis were in prison. Gandhi was an example to them all. For him jail was not a hardship but a crown of glory, for he knew that the capacity to suffer bravely for a higher ideal was the strength that would make every man and woman in India free. He embraced the prospect of imprisonment with such joy and good humor that people all over the country began to laugh off their own fear. British jails became the scenes of festive reunions as India's imprisoned political leaders found themselves joined by their families and friends. Gandhi sent them telegrams of congratulations. He himself was arrested so often that he seemed always to be either in prison, just released from prison, or about to be imprisoned again.

Gandhi was so detached from his physical environment that going to jail did not disrupt his work at all, and he drove some of his hardest bargains from behind jail walls. Usually the walls were those of Yeravda Prison, where he felt so much at home that once, when a British interrogator asked for his address, he answered, "Yeravda." When a man does everything in the spirit of worship, everywhere he goes is sacred, and Gandhi used to mark his jail letters *Yeravda Mandir,* which means "Yeravda temple." He started each day before dawn with meditation and prayer, in which he found the strength to withstand the trials of his situation. He was able to read the Bible, the Koran, and the Bhagavad Gita, and to conduct his usual voluminous correspondence every day. There was plenty of physical work to do, and plenty of would-be enemies, on both sides of the bars, to win over as friends. He looked after them all, even nursed them when they were ill, and every day he served in prison only added to his spiritual growth and made more converts to nonviolence and independence.

"There is no time-limit for a satyagrahi nor is there a limit to his capacity for suffering. Hence there is no such thing as defeat in satyagraha."

Visiting political

prisoners, 1939.

(Courtesy Jan Baros)

"Joy lies in the fight, in the attempt, in the suffering involved, not in the victory itself."

72

"I have learnt through bitter experience the one supreme lesson to conserve my anger, and as heat conserved is transmuted into energy, even so our anger controlled can be transmuted into a power which can move the world."

It is almost impossible to realize how much hatred and violence might have been unleashed in the struggle for political independence. India was seething with fury at Britain's exploitation, and wasted a great deal of its resistance in denouncing and declaiming, hating and trying to strike back. But Gandhi took this anger and put it to work in the fierce discipline of satyagraha, showing by his own example how it was possible to fight the British government nonviolently with every resource at his disposal and yet with complete love and respect for the British people. He knew that many of those who professed to follow him were incapable of such nonviolence. But if violence erupted from those seeking freedom, Gandhi suspended his offensive, even if success seemed imminent. He would not lead a satyagraha campaign without complete adherence to nonviolence.

Slowly, as British repression in India grew, the British people began to understand that by depriving Indians of political liberty they were not only harming India, they were harming Great Britain also. The finest young men that England could offer – soldiers and businessmen who, under other circumstances, could prove themselves capable of the highest courage and self-sacrifice – were drawn in India into the web of colonialist ways and grew callous toward those whom they claimed to govern, while the government of Great Britain was obliged to sacrifice more and more in human values to protect the lives and fortunes of such men. Because he knew that the English were as much his brothers and sisters as the Indians, no matter what their actions, Gandhi could turn to his exploiters and say: "We will not submit to this injustice – not merely because it is destroying us, but because it is destroying you as well." Gradually even high-placed British officials began to respond to this approach, and many British citizens came to Gandhi to work with him in his struggle for Indian self-help and self-rule.

"I believe that if one man gains spiritually the whole world gains with him and, if one man falls, the whole world falls to that extent. I do not help opponents without at the same time helping myself and my co-workers."

At tea with Lord Louis Mountbatten, India's last and most responsive viceroy, on the eve of independence.

(Courtesy Mr. Kulvant Roy)

Gandhi was in jail again when the British decided to convene a "round table conference" to decide India's fate. India's "representatives," invited by British crown officials, were the maharajas and politicians who were largely supported by the strength of British rule. Gandhi's American missionary friend Stanley Jones used to tell with great amusement how he was asked by Lord Irwin, the Viceroy of India, if Gandhi should be invited too. "Gandhi *is* India," Jones replied. "If you invite him, you invite India. If you do not, no matter whom else you do invite, all India will be absent." Lord Irwin, a little embarrassed, served Gandhi His Majesty's invitation in the cell at His Majesty's Yeravda Prison.

It was a far cry from the days when Gandhi was in London studying law. Now he was returning as a guest of the crown, representing one-fifth of the world's population. Yet when he arrived he turned down many grander arrangements to stay in one of the poorest sections of London, the East End. He captured the hearts of the people there, especially the children. He joked and played with them a little every day, no matter how busy his schedule, and they used to run after him in the fog on his long morning walks through the London slums, trying to keep up with his long strides and teasing him with cries of, "Hey, Gandhi, where's your pants?"

While he was in England Gandhi made a point of visiting Lancashire, where most of the British textile mills were located. Under colonial rule, India was required to export all its cotton at a nominal rate to England, where it was manufactured into cloth in the factories of Lancashire and sold back to the poor in India at many times the price they had been paid for growing it. Gandhi wanted all Indians, rich as well as poor, to learn the age-old craft of hand spinning so that the people of the seven hundred thousand impoverished villages of India could regain self-employment, self-reliance, and self-respect. He asked all Indians to wear the rough white homespun cloth called *khadi* and boycott foreign cloth. Khadi became the symbol of independence, linking the upper and middle classes of Indian society to the vast masses of the poor. Even great leaders like Jawaharlal Nehru spent some part of each day spinning khadi, and no one who supported independence, rich or poor, could dream of wearing anything else. While defenders of the empire like Sir Winston Churchill fumed, Gandhi wore his khadi loincloth and shawl even to tea at Buckingham Palace, with his ubiquitous dollar pocket watch suspended by a safety pin from his waist. "Mr. Gandhi," an English reporter asked him later, "don't you think you were a trifle under-dressed for the occasion?" "His Majesty," Gandhi answered, "had enough clothes on for both of us."

Greeting a crowd in London's East End from the balcony of the Quaker settlement house Kingsley Hall. (From the film *Mahatma*, by permission of Vithalbhai K. Jhaveri)

Eventually the textile mills of Lancashire had to declare a temporary shutdown. Thousands of British workers were thrown out of work, and Lancashire was full of unemployed millhands seething with resentment against Gandhi for having helped bring this about. But Gandhi knew that the English and Indian workers could understand each other if given the chance. Though the British government feared for his safety, he went to Lancashire to plead the cause of his people.

A great crowd of workers turned out to meet him, men and women, many of whom felt they had been thrown out of work by this one man. "Please listen to me for just a few minutes," Gandhi asked them quietly. "Give me a chance to present our point of view, and then, if you like, condemn me and my people. You tell me that three million people are out of employment here, have been out of employment for several months. In my country, three hundred million people are unemployed at least six months in every year. You say there are days when you can get only bread and butter for your dinner. But these people often go for days on end without any food at all." Such frank, respectful, but completely determined language won their admiration, and at the end of Gandhi's talk they all cheered him, the man who had brought about their unemployment.

"[Satyagraha] is a force that works silently and apparently slowly. In reality, there is no force in the world that is so direct or so swift in working."

With the same workers,

another view.

(From the film *Mahatma*, by

permission of Vithalbhai K.

Jhaveri)

"Nonviolence and cowardice go ill together. I can imagine a fully armed man to be at heart a coward. Possession of arms implies an element of fear, if not cowardice. But true nonviolence is an impossibility without the possession of unadulterated fearlessness."

It is easy, Gandhi used to say, for the strong person to become non-violent. It is the weakling who finds it impossible. For nonviolence means the capacity to love those who hate you, to show patience and understanding in the face of the most fiery opposition. This is the most difficult discipline one can learn in life, and that is why the Bhagavad Gita says that if you want to see the brave, look at those who can forgive. If you want to see the heroic, look at those who can love in return for hatred.

Nowhere was this transformation more vivid than in the North-west Frontier Province of India, among the rugged mountains of the Khyber Pass, where there arose a great leader who came to be known as the "Frontier Gandhi." Khan Abdul Ghaffar Khan came from a community where the law was "an eye for an eye and a tooth for a tooth." His people, the Pathans, are Muslims, brave, fierce fighters in whom the love of freedom burns strong. The British kept control of this strategic area through an often brutal military governance, but their hold was far from secure. The Frontier was a wild, mysterious place that seemed always ready to explode.

As soon as Gandhi launched his Salt Satyagraha, the Pathan Frontier was sealed off from the rest of India. Everyone expected the worst. But when reports began to trickle in, Gandhi was as astonished as anyone else to learn that Abdul Ghaffar Khan had answered the call to nonviolent action with the world's first nonviolent army. The Khudai Khidmatgars, "Servants of God," had sworn to nonviolence and forgiveness with Allah as their witness, and men, women, and children in the Frontier were facing even mass shootings without retreating or retaliating. Repression only inspired greater resistance. At the height of the struggle, the number of Khudai Khidmatgars was estimated at eighty to one hundred thousand.

At Khan's invitation, Gandhi decided to visit the Frontier. At each town, crowds of towering Pathans gathered. Many of them still

With Khan Abdul Ghaffar Khan.

(Courtesy Kanu Gandhi)

84

carried rifles slung over their shoulders, for a Pathan man considers himself undressed without his gun and knife. "Are you afraid?" Gandhi asked. "Why else would you be carrying guns?" They stared at him. No one had ever dared to speak to them like this. "I have taught myself not to be afraid of anyone," Gandhi explained; "that is why I am unarmed. This is what ahimsa means." The Pathans cheered him, and laid down their weapons to follow Abdul Ghaffar Khan. They were, Gandhi said, the perfect example of what he meant when he said that "nonviolence is the weapon of the brave."

"My creed of nonviolence is an extremely active force. It has no room for cowardice or even weakness. There is hope for a violent man to be some day nonviolent, but there is none for a coward."

"Strength does not come from physical capacity. It comes from an indomitable will."

Crossing a river on his peace mission through the remote area of Noakhali, East Bengal, during the Hindu-Muslim riots, 1946.
(By kind courtesy of
Hindusthan Standard,
Ananda Bazar Patrika, and
Desh group of newspapers)

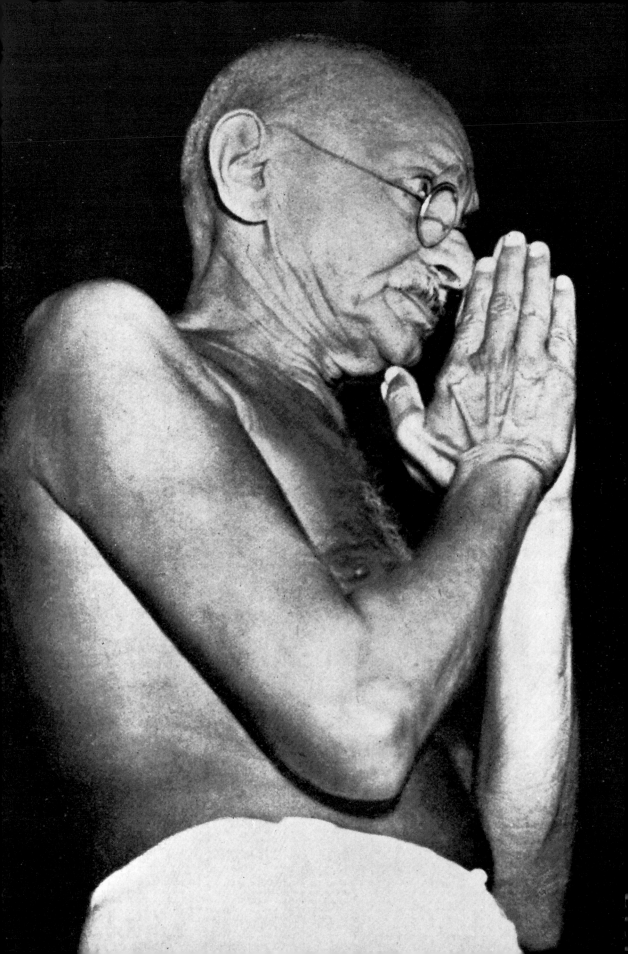

"Call it then by whatever name you like, that which gives one the greatest solace in the midst of the severest fire is God."

"Perfect love," the Bible says, "casts out fear." Ahimsa is perfect love. It is the farthest thing from mere sentimentality; it is a lifelong challenge, a lifelong battle within oneself, full of challenges and trials so severe that those who tread the path of love in every religious tradition have called it sharper than a razor's edge. Gandhi used to put the matter bluntly: when another person's welfare means more to you than your own, when even his life means more to you than your own, only then can you say you love. Anything else is just business, give-and-take. To extend this love even to those who hate you is the farthest limit of ahimsa. It pushes at the boundaries of consciousness itself.

Gandhi was a pioneer in these new realms of consciousness. Everything he did was an experiment in expanding the human being's capacity to love, and as his capacity grew, the demands on his love grew more and more severe, as if to test what limits a human being can bear. But Gandhi had learned to find a fierce joy in these storms and trials. Again and again, when the violence around him seemed impossible to face, he flung himself into the battle without thought of personal consolation or safety, and every time, at the eleventh hour, some deeper power within him would flood him with new reserves of energy and love. By the end of his life he was aflame with love. It burned in him night and day like a fire which nothing could quench, in which every lesser human consideration was consumed.

The challenges he faced toward the end of his life were among the greatest tragedies that history has seen. On the eve of independence, Hindu and Muslim India was in the throes of civil war. All the government forces were powerless to stop the massacres occurring almost daily on both sides. Gandhi, because he taught and lived the brotherhood of all religions, was hated intensely by many Hindus and Muslims alike.

The bloodshed and destruction touched the very depths of his being. Though in his mid-seventies he went straight to the heart of the violence and walked barefoot through the remote ravaged villages of Bihar state and Noakhali as a one-man force for peace,

The traditional Hindu greeting with which Gandhi blessed his assassin.

(Courtesy Jan Baros)

*Passing through a
village in Bihar during
the riots, accompanied
by Khan Abdul
Ghaffar Khan.*

(Jagan V. Mehta)

dependent even for his food on the mercy of his enemies. Some of his
most trusted followers, who had been tested in other campaigns and
could be counted on not to falter in their courage and their love, he
sent alone to other villages to follow his example. They had no
instructions but to live the truths they went to teach: love and respect
for all persons, complete self-reliance, and the utter fearlessness of
ahimsa.

90

"He who trembles or takes to his heels the moment he sees two people fighting is not nonviolent, but a coward. A nonviolent person will lay down his life in preventing such quarrels."

Inspecting a wrecked house during the riots in Bihar.

(Courtesy Braj Kishore Sinha)

"Strength of numbers is the delight of the timid. The valiant in spirit glory in fighting alone."

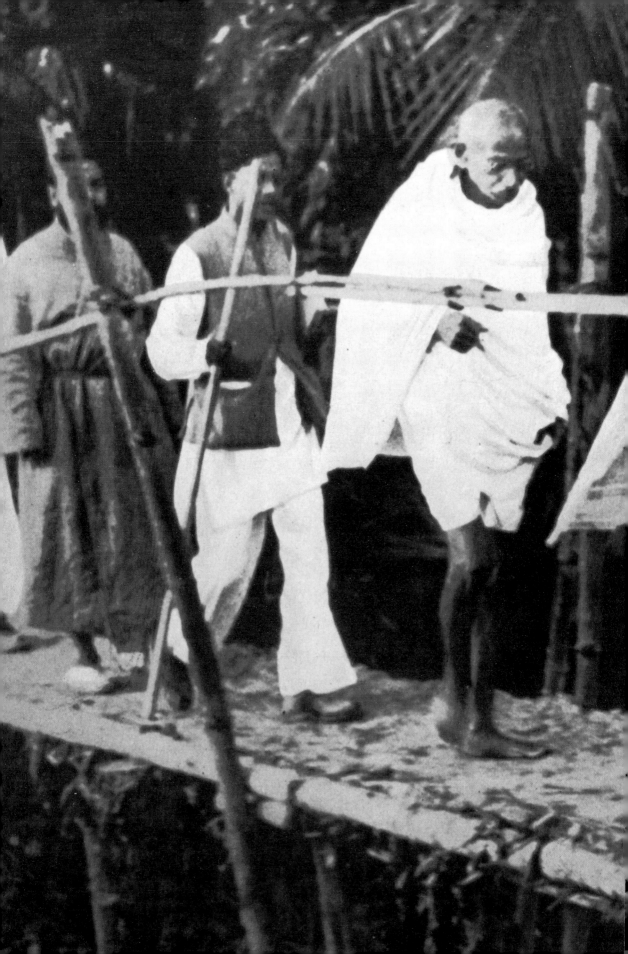

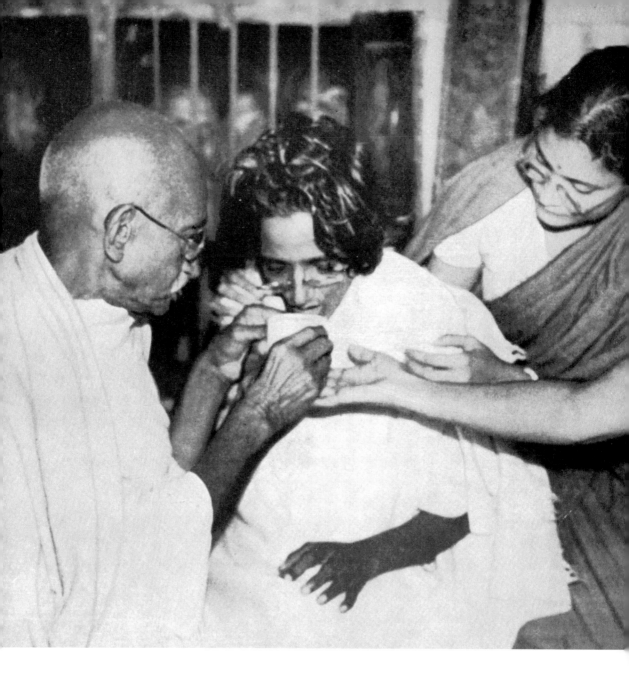

Helping Amtus Salaam, a young Muslim disciple, break a successful twenty-five-day fast undertaken to bring Hindus and Muslims together in the village in Noakhali to which Gandhi had sent her alone.

(By kind courtesy of *Hindusthan Standard*, *Ananda Bazar Patrika*, and *Desh* group of newspapers)

For Gandhi it was the acid test of ahimsa, and every resource in him flared up to meet the demand. He walked, worked, wrote, and spoke sixteen to twenty hours a day. Everywhere he went, by his personal example, he dissolved the barriers erected by religious customs, superstition, and mistrust. In each community some small miracle would occur: Muslim families took the risk of giving him shelter; murderers and looters came forward to give him their weapons, return what they had taken, or offer him money for the relief of the dispossessed. In one village, it is said, a notoriously fierce communal agitator came up to Gandhi in front of a crowd of paralyzed onlookers, put his hands around Gandhi's slender throat, and began choking the life out of him. Such is the height to which Gandhi had grown that there was not even a flicker of hostility in his eyes, not a word of protest. He yielded himself completely to the flood of love within him, and the man broke down like a little child and fell sobbing at his feet. For those who watched, it seemed a miracle. For Gandhi, who had grown used to the "miracles" of love, it only proved for the hundredth time in his own life the depth of the words of the Compassionate Buddha: "Hatred does not cease by hatred at any time; hatred ceases by love. This is an unalterable law."

"Devotion is not mere lip-worship, it is a wrestling with death."

"Policies may and do change. Nonviolence is an unchangeable creed. It has to be pursued in face of violence raging around you."

"Nonviolence with a nonviolent man is no merit. In fact it becomes difficult to say whether it is nonviolence at all. But when it is pitted against violence, then one realizes the difference between the two. This we cannot do unless we are ever wakeful, ever vigilant, ever striving."

A Muslim woman in Bihar, whose belongings were destroyed by a mob, appealing to Gandhi for help.

(Jagan V. Mehta)

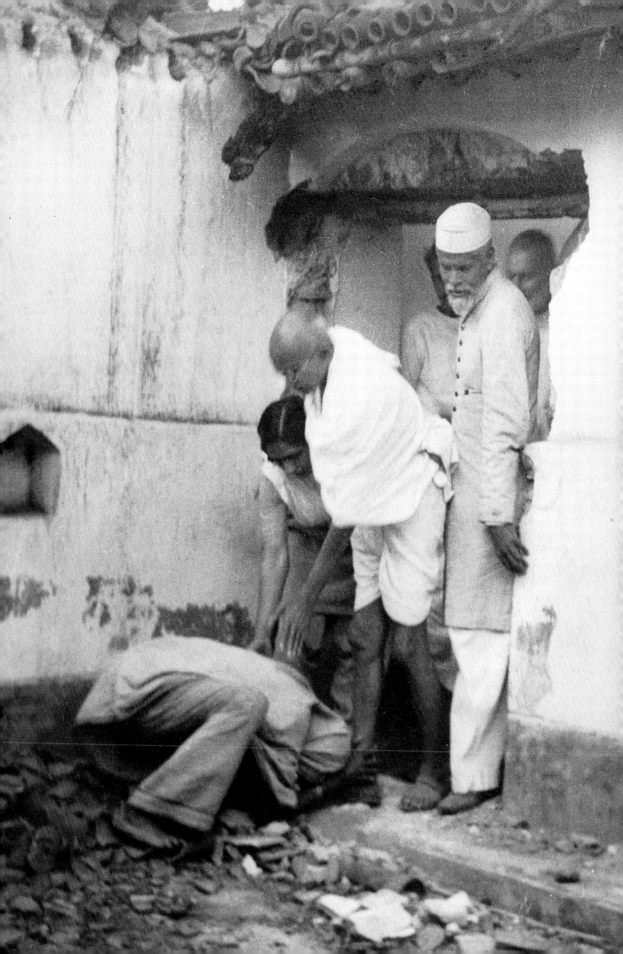

"Have I that nonviolence of the brave in me? My death alone will show that. If someone killed me and I died with prayer for the assassin on my lips, and God's remembrance and consciousness of His living presence in the sanctuary of my heart, then alone would I be said to have had the nonviolence of the brave."

In Bihar.

(Jagan V. Mehta)

Morning walk during
Gandhi's peace mission
in Bihar, accompanied
by Khan Abdul Ghaffar
Khan. (Jagan V. Mehta)

"*The goal ever recedes from us. The greater the progress the greater the recognition of our unworthiness. Satisfaction lies in the effort, not in the attainment. Full effort is full victory.*"

In rare seclusion at the home of the wealthy industrialist G.D. Birla, where the last prayer meeting was held on January 30, 1948. (Henri Cartier-Bresson, Magnum)

Mother & Child

Activists and scholars have studied what they call "Gandhian politics" and "Gandhian economics," but few have asked the questions which really count. How did he do it? From what did he draw his strength? How did such an ordinary little man, an ineffectual lawyer without a purpose, manage to transform himself into someone able to stand and fight alone against the greatest empire the world has known, and win – without firing a shot?

One American journalist who had been following Gandhi's work for years with mounting admiration finally asked him with the terseness of a newsman: "Can you tell me the secret of your life in three words?"

"Yes!" chuckled Gandhi, who could never resist a challenge. "'Renounce and enjoy'!"

Gandhi was quoting from the Isha Upanishad, one of the most ancient of the Hindu scriptures. For him the whole of the Bhagavad Gita was only a commentary on these three simple words, which encompass the summit of human wisdom. They mean that in order to enjoy life, we cannot be selfishly attached to anything – money, possessions, power or prestige, even family or friends. The moment we are selfishly attached, we become their prisoner.

"By detachment I mean that you must not worry whether the desired result follows from your action or not, so long as your motive is pure, your means correct. Really, it means that things will come right in the end if you take care of the means and leave the rest to Him."

In the language of the Bhagavad Gita, detachment is "skillfulness in action." A person who is worried about the outcome of his work does not see his goal; he sees only his opposition and the obstacles before him. Feeling unequal to the difficulties of his situation, he becomes resigned or resorts to violence out of frustration and despair. But the person who is detached from results and tries only to do his best without thought of profit or power or prestige does not waver when difficulties come. He sees his way clearly through every trial, for his eyes are always on the goal.

Detachment is not apathy or indifference. It is the prerequisite for effective involvement. Often what we think is best for others is distorted by our attachment to our opinions: we want others to be happy in the way we think they should be happy. It is only when we want nothing for ourselves that we are able to see clearly into others' needs and understand how to serve them.

While he was pursuing his own career Gandhi had no access to the immense storehouse of creativity which lies within. It was only when he began to live for others that he found himself bursting with almost unharnessable power. By the time he was in his seventies his capacity for work was several times what it had been in his twenties, and in periods of intense crisis, which grew more and more frequent as his dedication deepened, he rose to even greater heights of energy and endurance. During the Round Table Conference he never got to bed before eleven at night and he woke up again at two in the morning. On his pilgrimage through the regions of Noakhali and Bihar during the Hindu-Muslim riots, at the age of seventy-seven, the schedule was the same. But because he had learned not to worry about success or failure he could give all his attention to the work at hand, without feeling the burdens of anxiety or fatigue.

"Mr. Gandhi," a Western journalist asked him once, "you have been working at least fifteen hours a day, every day, for almost fifty years. Don't you think it's about time you took a vacation?"

"Why?" Gandhi said. "I am always on vacation."

It is the Bhagavad Gita which teaches most clearly this art of living in freedom. Gandhi is first and last a child of the Gita. No amount of study of his work in politics, economics, or nonviolent resistance can reveal the real source of his power. But Gandhi himself tells us with the profound simplicity of a child:

> *"The Gita has been a mother to me ever since I became first acquainted with it in 1889. I turn to it for guidance in every difficulty, and the desired guidance has always been forthcoming. But you must approach Mother Gita in all reverence, if you would benefit by her ministrations. One who rests his head on her peace-giving lap never experiences disappointment but enjoys bliss in perfection. This spiritual mother gives her devotee fresh knowledge, hope and power every moment of his life."*

It is one thing to translate the Gita into another language and quite a different thing to translate it into daily living. The first is an intellectual exercise on the surface level of the personality, no matter how much talent and scholarship may be involved. The second reaches into the utmost depths of consciousness and leads to the complete transformation of character and conduct.

In London during the Second Round Table Conference, 1930.

(From the film Mahatma, by permission of Vithalbhai K. Jhaveri)

If we can understand the Bhagavad Gita as a manual for daily living, we can understand Gandhi. But it is not possible to comprehend the Gita in this way without trying, as Gandhi did, to put it into practice.

"It is no nonviolence if we merely love those that love us. It is nonviolence only when we love those that hate us. I know how difficult it is to follow this grand law of love. But are not all great and good things difficult to do? Love of the hater is the most difficult of all. But by the grace of God even this most difficult thing becomes easy to accomplish if we want to do it."

"I have not been able to see any difference between the Sermon on the Mount and the Bhagavad Gita. What the Sermon describes in a graphic manner, the Bhagavad Gita reduces to a scientific formula. It may not be a scientific book in the accepted sense of the term, but it has argued out the law of love – the law of abandon as I would call it – in a scientific manner."

With the Muslim leader Mohammed Ali Jinnah in Bombay in 1944.
(Courtesy of *Hindusthan Standard, Ananda Bazar Patrika,* and *Desh* group of newspapers)

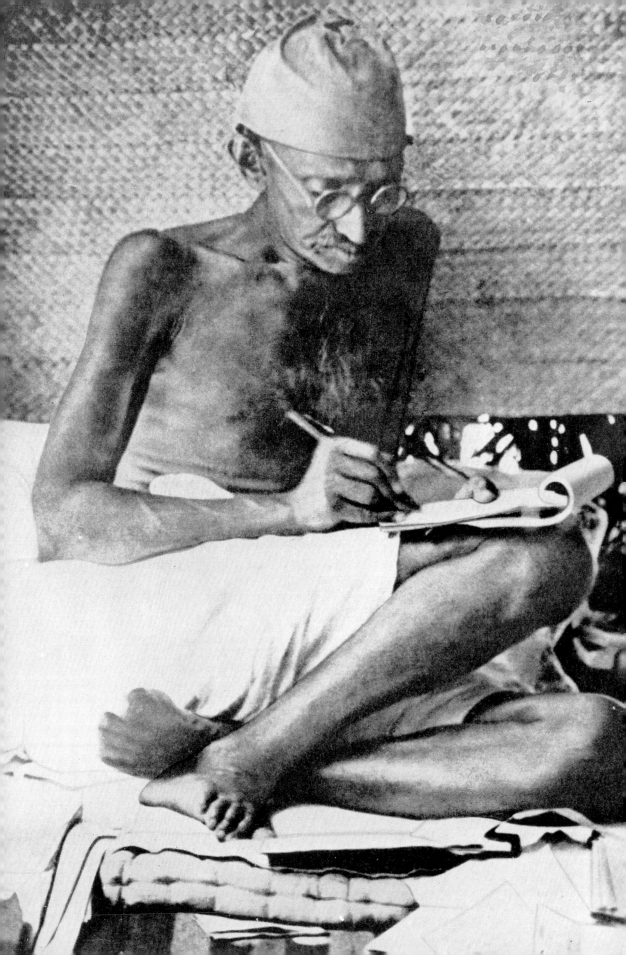

"*The Gita says: 'Do your allotted work, but renounce its fruit – be detached and work – have no desire for reward and work.'*

"*This is the unmistakable teaching of the Gita. He who gives up action falls. He who gives up only the reward rises. But renunciation of fruit in no way means indifference to the result. In regard to every action one must know the result that is expected to follow, the means thereto, and the capacity for it. He, who, being thus equipped, is without desire for the result, and is yet wholly engrossed in the due fulfillment of the task before him, is said to have renounced the fruits of his action.*"

In 1942.

(Courtesy Kanu Gandhi)

On the train.

(Courtesy Kanu Gandhi)

"A true votary of the Gita does not know what disappointment is. He ever dwells in perennial joy and peace that passeth understanding. But that peace and joy come not to the skeptic or to him who is proud of his intellect or learning. It is reserved only for the humble in spirit, who bring to her worship a fullness of faith and an undivided singleness of mind."

"Undivided singleness of mind" is what the Gita means by yoga. It is the complete opposite of the incessant civil warfare among intellect, senses, emotions, and instincts which is our usual state of mind. Yoga is the complete reintegration of all these fragments on every level of the personality. It is the process of becoming whole.

During the Round Table Conference in London Gandhi lived the cause of Indian freedom every waking moment of his day. It was a spontaneous appeal which had an immediate effect on the British people because Gandhi identified so completely with his message. He did not have to plan speeches or stage events; everything he did embodied what he believed.

On one occasion during the conference Gandhi spoke eloquently before the assembled delegates for over two hours on behalf of the people of India. After he had finished, the London reporters clustered excitedly around Gandhi's secretary, Mahadev Desai. "How is it," they demanded, "that he is able to speak so well for such a long time without any preparation, without any prompting, without even any notes?" Desai replied, "What Gandhi thinks, what he feels, what he says, and what he does are all the same. He does not need notes." Then he added smiling: "You and I, we think one thing, feel another, say a third, and do a fourth, so we need notes and files to keep track."

"At the time of writing I never think of what I have said before. My aim is not to be consistent with my previous statements on a given question, but to be consistent with truth as it may present itself to me at a given moment. The result has been that I have grown from truth to truth; I have saved my memory an undue strain; and what is more, whenever I have been obliged to compare my writing even of fifty years ago with the latest, I have discovered no inconsistency between the two."

In Noakhali, 1946.

(Courtesy Kanu Gandhi)

"*There comes a time when an individual becomes irresistible and his action becomes all-pervasive in its effect. This comes when he reduces himself to zero.*"

On his morning walk at Juhu Beach, Bombay, recovering from an illness incurred in prison, 1944. Kasturbai and Mahadev Desai had both died in prison shortly before.

(Datta Khopker)

Very few of us see life as it really is. Most of us see things only as we are, looking at others through our own likes and dislikes, prejudices and prepossessions, desires, interests, and fears. It is this separatist outlook that fragments life for us – person against person, community against community, nation against nation. In order to see life as it is, one undivided whole, we have to shed all attachment to personal profit, power, pleasure, or prestige. Otherwise we cannot help looking at life through our individual conditioning, and we will see the world not as it is, but as conditioned by our desires.

Through many years of such conditioning, trying again and again to satisfy the desire for personal satisfaction, we have come to believe that this is our real personality. In reality it is a mask which we have merely forgotten how to take off. Beneath the mask is all the glory of our real self: complete fearlessness, unconditioned love, and abiding joy. When Gandhi succeeded in taking off this mask and "making himself zero" through many years of living for others rather than himself, he found that what he had eliminated from his personality was only his separateness, his selfishness, his fear. What remained was the love and fearlessness that had been hidden there all the time.

A teacher of meditation in ancient India, Patanjali, says that in the presence of a man in whom all hostility has died, because he does not challenge anyone, others cannot be hostile. In the presence of a man in whom all fear has died, because he does not threaten anyone, no one can be afraid. It is a precise, scientific definition of what power is released in true ahimsa.

"For a nonviolent person, the whole world is one family. He will thus fear none, nor will others fear him."

One evening at the Sevagram ashram hundreds of people had gathered for the nightly prayer meeting. The sun was about to set and it was the time when snakes begin to come out after the fierce heat of the Indian day. This evening a cobra was seen gliding toward the gathering. A cobra's bite is swift and deadly, and in the villages of India, where medical help is usually far away, such snakes strike terror into everyone. A ripple of panic began to sweep through the crowd, and there was danger that some might be trampled if the terror spread. But Gandhi quietly showed a sign not to move.

Gandhi was seated on the platform. He wore only his dhoti or loincloth; legs, chest, and arms were bare. While the crowd held its breath and watched, the cobra made straight for Gandhi and slowly began to crawl over his thighs.

There was a long moment of silence in which no one dared to move or make a sound. Gandhi must have been repeating his mantram, *Rama, Rama, Rama*. Even the cobra lost all trace of fear. In

its own way it must have sensed it was in the presence of someone who would never cause it suffering. Slowly, quietly it crawled away, leaving everyone unharmed.

"The simplest things have the knack sometimes of appearing to us the hardest. If our hearts were opened, we should have no difficulty.

"Nonviolence is a matter of the heart. It does not come to us through any intellectual feat. Everyone has faith in God though everyone does not know it. For, everyone has faith in himself and that multiplied to the nth degree is God."

With a Muslim boy in Bihar, 1947.

(Jagan V. Mehta)

Fearlessness was not something Gandhi was born with. Even in high school, he had been terrified of boys much less his size. He had only a budding capacity for endurance and a deep, driving desire to make himself strong.

An old family servant, Rambha, was the first to come to his aid. "There is nothing wrong in admitting you are afraid," she assured him. "But whenever something threatens you, instead of running away, hold your ground and repeat the mantram *Rama, Rama* over and over again in your mind. It can turn your fear into fearlessness."

Because he loved her Gandhi followed Rambha's suggestion for a while, but soon he forgot it again. To his young mind, growing up in an atmosphere of Western education, repeating a mantram must have sounded mechanical and superstitious. But Gandhi was too much a scientist to believe or disbelieve in something for very long without experimenting with it for himself. The seed Rambha had sown deep in his consciousness continued to grow throughout his childhood, and finally, when the storms of conflict and racial hatred began to break over him in South Africa, the mantram came to him again from deep within. Gradually, as it verified itself in his life, the mantram became his greatest support, an infallible source of strength.

"The mantram becomes one's staff of life and carries one through every ordeal...."

"Each repetition ... has a new meaning, each repetition carries you nearer and nearer to God."

A mantram is a spiritual formula which seekers from all traditions have found can transform what is negative in the personality into what is positive: anger into compassion, ill will into good will, hatred into love. By calming the mind, it gradually integrates divided and opposing thoughts at a deeper and deeper level of consciousness.

Rama, Gandhi's mantram, is a formula for abiding joy. Gandhi used to walk for miles every day repeating it to himself until the rhythm of the mantram and his footsteps began to stabilize the rhythm of his breathing, which is closely connected with the rhythm of the mind. When fear or anger threatened him, clinging to *Rama* used the power of these emotions to drive this formula for joy deep into Gandhi's mind. Falling asleep in *Rama, Rama*, he fell asleep in joy. Over the years, as the mantram penetrated below his deepest doubts and fears, he became established in joy. It was a habit of mind which no surface turbulence could shake, no threat of violence destroy.

Many times while he was growing up, Gandhi's nurse Rambha must have taken him to see the temple elephants going in procession on holy days through the narrow, crooked streets of the Porbandar bazaar, weaving their way between the rows of vegetable and fruit stands on either side. In her devout eyes these elephants were a vivid illustration of what the mantram *Rama* can do. As they go through the streets among the shops, their trunks writhe restlessly from side to side like snakes, dipping into every stall for coconuts and bananas by the bunch to throw into their cavernous mouths. No threats or promises can make them settle down. But a skillful mahout, who knows and loves his elephant well, just gives it a bamboo stick for its trunk to hold. The moment the trunk wraps itself around the bamboo, it settles down. There is no restlessness, no pilfering. The elephant walks through the crowded streets with its head held high, holding the bamboo before it proudly, paying not the slightest attention to the coconuts and bananas on either side.

"Your mind," Rambha would tell little Mohandas, "is very much like that elephant's trunk. When it takes hold of the mantram, all its restlessness falls away." It is the same message as that of the Bhagavad Gita: Make your mind steady in every circumstance – victory and defeat, praise and blame, love and hatred – and wherever you go, nothing can shake you from your goal. Then you can call yourself free.

The mantram calms the mind and prepares it for meditation, which is the key to this transformation of character and consciousness. Meditation is not a religion. It is a dynamic discipline independent of any belief or dogma, in which all one's powers of concentration are brought to bear upon one overriding ideal to drive it deep into the mind, until it gradually consumes all smaller ideals and goals. Through this discipline one enters the deepest levels of con-

sciousness, where the storms of deep-seated conflicts rage continuously night and day. It is at these awesome depths, as Gandhi put it, that love wrestles with anger and fear "and ultimately gains mastery over all other feelings."

The principle of meditation is that you become what you meditate on. Gandhi meditated "with an undivided singleness of mind" on the ideal of the Bhagavad Gita: the man who renounces everything for love of serving others, and lives in freedom and joy.

At a prayer meeting.

(Courtesy Kanu Gandhi)

119

"The last eighteen verses of the Second Chapter of the Gita give in a nutshell the secret of the art of living."

"[Those] verses of the Second Chapter have since been inscribed on the tablet of my heart. They contain for me all knowledge. The truths they teach me are the 'eternal verities.' There is reasoning in them, but they represent realized knowledge.

"I have since read many translations and many commentaries, have argued and reasoned to my heart's content, but the impression that the first reading gave me has never been effaced. Those verses are the key to the interpretation of the Gita."

Portrait.

(D. R. D. Wadia)

The second chapter of the Bhagavad Gita ends with a description of the highest state of consciousness a human being can attain. It is the fullest expression of the Gita ideal. When your love is deep enough, Sri Krishna has been telling Arjuna, every selfish attachment falls away, and with it all frustration, all insecurity, all despair. Arjuna asks enthusiastically: "How can I recognize such a person when I see him? What are the marks of the man who lives always in wisdom, completely established in himself? Tell me how he talks, how he acts, how he conducts himself when under attack." And Krishna replies:

> They live in wisdom
> Who see themselves in all and all in them,
> Whose love for the Lord of Love has consumed
> Every selfish desire and sense-craving
> Tormenting the heart. Not agitated
> By grief nor hankering after pleasure,
> They live free from lust and fear and anger.
> Fettered no more by selfish attachments,
> They are not elated by good fortune
> Nor depressed by bad. Such are the seers....
>
> When you keep thinking about sense-objects,
> Attachment comes. Attachment breeds desire,
> The lust of possession which, when thwarted,
> Burns to anger. Anger clouds the judgment
> And robs you of the power to learn from past
> Mistakes. Lost is the discriminative
> Faculty, and your life is utter waste.
>
> But when you move amidst the world of sense
> From both attachment and aversion freed,
> There comes the peace in which all sorrows end,
> And you live in the wisdom of the Self.
>
> The disunited mind is far from wise;
> How can it meditate? How be at peace?

When you know no peace, how can you know joy?
When you let your mind follow the siren
Call of the senses, they carry away
Your better judgment as a cyclone drives
A boat off the charted course to its doom....

They are forever free who have bɩɔken
Out of the ego-cage of *I* and *mine*
To be united with the Lord of Love.
This is the supreme state. Attain thou this
And pass from death to immortality.

These are the verses which summarize Gandhi's life. For more than fifty years he meditated on them morning and night and devoted all his effort to translating them, with the help of the mantram, into his daily action. They are the key to his self-transformation.

Gandhi the Man

The American journalist Louis Fischer had followed Gandhi's campaigns in India for many years, and had learned to wonder at the practical wisdom of this little man who was so successfully applying the laws of love to the turbulent challenges of power politics. But when at last he had the opportunity to visit Gandhi at home, it was not Gandhi the politician who captured his heart, it was Gandhi the man: his endless vitality, his warmth, his gentle, unshakable strength, his never-failing sense of humor and infectious joy. Here was a man who had almost no possessions, but was rich in inner experience; who seemed to suffer endless calamities and setbacks, but never lost his resilience and good temper; who had just six or seven books on his desk, but was full of practical wisdom.

Fischer spent a week with Gandhi, seeing him every day, walking with him, sharing his meals, captivated, like hundreds of other such visitors, by what he called "the miracle of personality." When he left, it was with a lingering sense that Gandhi's most important experiments were not in politics at all, but in the art of living meaningfully in a world full of violent conflict and incessant change.

"People should think less about what they ought to do," said the medieval German mystic Meister Eckhart, "and more about what they ought to be. If only their living were good, their work would shine forth brightly." Gandhi thought only about what he should be, and everything he did shone with beauty. To those who met him, even many who came as enemies, he was the supreme artist who had made the smallest detail of his life a work of art.

At a prayer meeting.

(Datta Khopker)

"My life is an indivisible whole, and all my activities run into one another; and they all have their rise in my insatiable love of mankind."

125

It was his wife, Gandhi admitted later, who taught him how to love. By her personal example, Kasturbai showed the way to root out the anger and competition eroding their marriage: not by retaliating and inflaming the situation more, but by constantly trying to support him and bear with him through his outbursts and mistakes, keeping her eyes always on what was good in him and encouraging him silently to live up to her respect. Gradually Gandhi began to see that she was practicing every day what he himself had been admiring as a theoretical ideal. He took up her example, and each became the other's teacher as Gandhi learned Kasturbai's patience and inspired her with his own fiery enthusiasm in return. It was a long, arduous, exacting discipline, which he used to say required the patience of a man trying to empty the sea with a cup. But every time they overcame a barrier between them, they found they were not only able to love each other more, they had more love and patience for everyone else as well. By the time Gandhi had learned to bring this love to bear even on his enemies, Kasturbai too was in prison, gathering other women to her leadership.

Gandhi did not expect those who came to him to make this transformation immediately, or reverse overnight the conditioning of millions of years of evolution and love their enemies more than they loved themselves. He himself had failed countless times in his attempts to reach that highest state. "Start where you are," he used to tell them. "If you can't love the Viceroy, or Sir Winston Churchill, start with your wife, or your husband, or your children. Try to put their welfare first and your own last every minute of the day, and let the circle of your love expand from there. As long as you are trying your very best, there can be no question of failure." This is the discipline by which Gandhi built his capacity for satyagraha. It is the deepest motivation a human being can tap, for it answers directly the deepest human need: the need to love.

Kasturbai in 1934, at the age of sixty-five.

(Courtesy Sarvodaya Diwas Samiti)

"Love never claims, it ever gives. Love ever suffers, never resents, never revenges itself."

"We have to make truth and nonviolence not matters for mere individual practice but for practice by groups and communities and nations. That at any rate is my dream. I shall live and die in trying to realize it. My faith helps me to discover new truths every day.

"Ahimsa is the attribute of the soul, and, therefore, to be practiced by everybody in all the affairs of life. If it cannot be practiced in all departments, it has no practical value."

In the course of his life, Gandhi created a number of communities or ashrams where men, women, and children from all backgrounds and nationalities came to learn from his daily example how to make non-violence and love the basis of their lives. In the early stages of the movement in India people came to him at Sabarmati for this training, across from the bleak textile mills of Ahmedabad. This was his home for fifteen years. From Sabarmati he launched the movement for homespun cloth and the Salt Satyagraha of 1930. When his work called him elsewhere, Gandhi gave the ashram at Sabarmati over to Harijan service and later went to live in a village in central India to make his home among the people there. The ashram that grew up around him was called Sevagram, which means the "village of service."

Gandhi carefully chose the site for Sevagram a few miles from Wardha, the nearest train junction, in a part of India which is unbearably hot. Most Indians had to live in this climate, and that is why he preferred it for his ashram rather than a cool Himalayan hill station or a fertile tract along the Ganges. He may have hoped for isolation, but in a few years there were so many people walking to the ashram that by their feet they made a road. He received so much mail that the government was obliged to open a post office there. So many telegrams came that a telegraph office was set up. Sevagram became a throbbing beehive of activity, where all the world could see what it means to do even the smallest daily acts in love.

Leaving his hut at

Sevagram.

(Courtesy Kanu Gandhi)

"You must watch my life, how I live, eat, sit, talk, behave in general. The sum total of all those in me is my religion."

Gandhi's day began very early, around three or four, to take advantage of the cool and quiet of the Indian morning. This is the time of day when the mind is naturally most at peace, and even in the midst of the most pressing national crisis, whether he was in London or on a train or in a cell in one of "His Majesty's hotels," Gandhi never failed to use this time for meditation. It was the most essential part of his day, much more so than his meals; for every morning it released a new flood of energy which renewed every cell of his body. Throughout the rest of the day he would draw on these early morning hours for patience, courage, resilience, and an irrepressible good humor.

When his meditation was over, Gandhi plunged into the business of the day. Every minute was given over to others, beginning with the steady stream of visitors who came from all over the world for every conceivable reason: to get an interview for the *New York Times,* to settle some question of Harijan voting rights, to argue with his opinions on birth control or to get help in disciplining an unruly child. Beyond those who requested interviews stood the mute crowds who had come just to watch this "poor little man of Sevagram" who had made the smallest detail of his life a joy to watch. With Gandhi, who was at home with himself wherever he went, they immediately felt at home: as if they had always belonged at Sevagram, and Gandhi's huge adopted family were their own. Gandhi gave each one his attention, fitting them somehow into his own close schedule for the day: talking to them on his morning walk, or at breakfast, or over the spinning wheel. He had not the slightest privacy; everything he did was observed by strangers, so that his life was beautifully transparent. Once his co-worker Mary Barr wrote to apologize for having accidentally intruded on him the day before and disturbed, she thought, some stolen moment of solitude and quiet. "You did not disturb my solitude," Gandhi wrote back. "My solitude is taken in the midst of many."

In the middle of all this apparent chaos Gandhi kept order by an

exacting attention to detail and to time. He was punctual to the
minute and expected everyone who came to him, even the most
important British minister, to measure up to his own demanding
standards. "You may not waste a grain of rice or a scrap of paper," he

Playing with a child.

(Courtesy Kanu Gandhi)

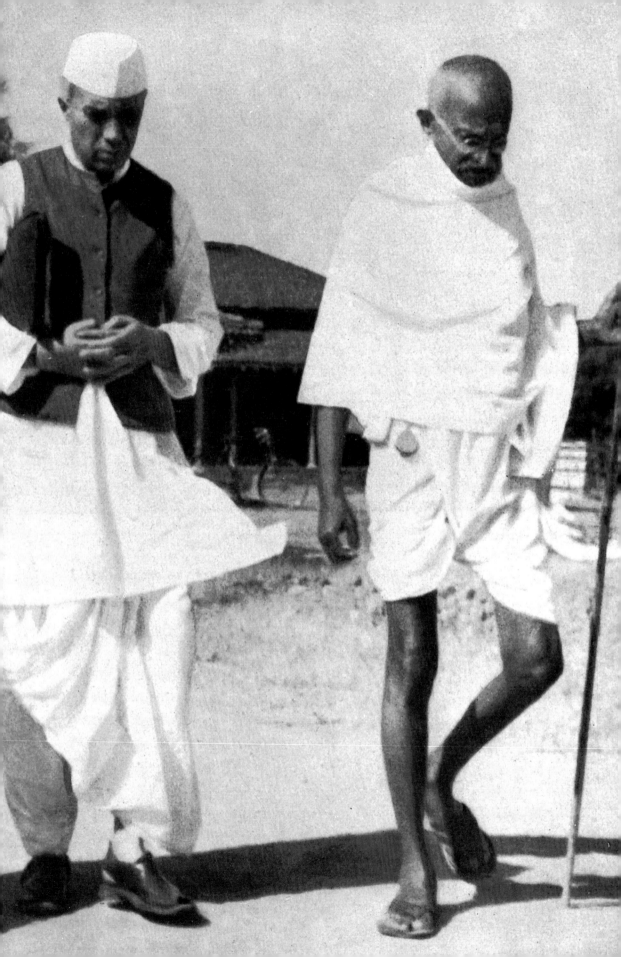

wrote, "and similarly a minute of your time. It is not ours. It belongs to the nation and we are trustees for the use of it."

Often, too, in those turbulent years, much of the day's business was fraught with pressure and tension, and it was not uncommon to see Jawaharlal Nehru or one of the other great Indian political leaders suddenly show up at Sevagram from the far side of the continent, burdened with problems affecting several hundred million lives. Usually it was only minutes before such visitors found themselves chuckling in spite of themselves at one of Gandhi's jokes, and when they left, by some alchemy of personality, they would be relaxed again, full of new enthusiasm and inspirations ready to take on their problems with a clear perspective and deeper strength. Punctuating these great national crises was the incessant pattern of local problems and tragedies: a disease among the cattle, a child dying of pneumonia, a man from some nearby village seeking Gandhi's permission to leave his wife. And behind all these matters hung the vast problem of the Indian poor, whom Gandhi had the daily responsibility for leading to self-sufficiency and self-rule. He moved through such trials with the grace of a dancer, always cheerful, always gentle, as serene and as deep as the sea of peace described in the Bhagavad Gita, into which the most turbulent rivers empty and are stilled.

LEFT:

With Jawaharlal Nehru at Sevagram, 1939.

(Courtesy Sumati Morarjee and Vithalbhai K. Jhaveri)

THIS PAGE:

With Nehru, 1946.

(Courtesy Sarvodaya Diwas Samiti)

But it was when he was with his ashram family that Gandhi's beauty shone most clearly. It was an odd collection: men, women, and children from all parts of the world, so varied in their backgrounds and dispositions that Sardar Vallabhbhai Patel, Gandhi's brusque companion from the earliest days of Indian satyagraha, used to refer laughingly to the "ashram menagerie." Everywhere Gandhi went he attracted men and women whose love for him released tremendous reserves of loyalty, courage, and selfless service which utterly transformed their lives. Even in South Africa, as his conception of "family" expanded, such people had joined his household and devoted themselves completely to his way of life. Many of them were women, who responded deeply to his unique understanding of their quiet, tough, patient strength, their selflessness, their capacity to forgive. "If nonviolence is the law of our being," he said of them admiringly, "the future is with woman." He took them all into his family, and because he had learned to extend his love for Kasturbai and their children to everyone else as well, there always seemed to be room for one more. The whole world was his family. Once, when a reporter asked Kasturbai how many children she had, she told him playfully: "I have four. But Bapu, my husband, has four hundred million."

There is no more beautiful aspect of Gandhi's character than his loving relationship with each one of people who were part of his ashram family. He was concerned with every detail of their lives, and while he demanded a great deal from those close to him, his treatment of them was filled with love, humor, and tact. His relationship with each person was individual. He was conscious of the needs of others even to the smallest detail, and often overwhelmed people near him by observing and attending to some minute need of theirs in the midst of his own busy schedule. No detail of ashram life escaped his notice, and he loved to make his rounds in the afternoon, taking time to joke and play with the children and see how work was going in the kitchen. The ashram sick were his special love; he vented on them all his childhood passion for nursing, and visited each person in the Sevagram infirmary with some special little gift or bit of news. It was always a cheerful scene when Gandhi was around. In an account of one of his visits to Gandhi, Louis Fischer tells of waking

up one morning to the sound of one of the ashram women singing to herself like a teenager in the next room. When she came out onto the veranda he asked her why she had been singing. "Because I am happy," she replied.

"And why are you happy?"

She smiled. "We are happy because we are near Bapu."

Dinner at Sevagram, for the uninitiated, was often full of surprises. Gandhi had little interest in gourmet fare; for him the body was an instrument of service, and he gave it food the same way he would give an engine gas. "Eat only what you need," he advised, "only when you

With his grandnieces Manubehn Gandhi and Mrs. Abha Gandhi, who were at his side during his last days.

(UPI)

135

are hungry, and only when you have done at least a little work for others." Then, too, ever since his student years in London he had been experimenting with every possible vegetarian combination with a laughing disregard for the esthetics of his menus. At times the results were outlandish, and it was usually a favorite guest whom Gandhi would choose to show the dubious favor of sharing his latest soup or chutney, full of obscure vitamins and sometimes bitter as gall. To Gandhi it was enough that the dish was nutritious; knowing that made it taste good too.

Meals at the ashram had the intimacy of a family sacrament. Gandhi knew that even the most wholesome meal needs to be cooked and eaten with love, and he kept those around him in the best of spirits with just the right touch of jokes and friendly questions. He talked very little, but to everything worthy of interest he gave his complete concentration. Even in such little matters he was teaching his family by personal example to keep all their attention on the work at hand, so that in the heat of a campaign neither anger nor fear would be able to sweep them away.

After dinner all national business ended and a crowd gathered for what looked like a procession to accompany Gandhi on his evening walk. By then the terrible heat of the Central Indian sun had abated a little, and it would have been a great blessing for Gandhi to have had this one hour of the day to himself. Instead he chose to give more time to those who wanted to talk or ask him questions, and, when these were silent, to provoke a little more laughter from the ashram children. But though he was in his seventies he still walked very fast, and after a while the procession dwindled as more and more people dropped behind. He was so light that his body hardly held him down at all; his feet scarcely touched the earth and he seemed almost to be flying.

In the evening after his walk the prayer meeting was held under the tropical sky. As the sun set, hundreds of people gathered around with hurricane lanterns to hear Gandhi speak. There was a lot of noise, and the crowd swayed and moved like the sea.

When Gandhi came he seemed small and frail, yet his presence was

commanding. He barely raised his hand as a signal. Everyone became still, all eyes fixed on the little figure seated on the platform.

His voice was gentle and sweet. It seemed soft but it carried far. In the first few minutes of his talk Gandhi absorbed the feeling of the audience and its needs. His words came slowly and precisely; so like a child was he that it was possible to see his thoughts arise, develop, and be articulated in simple but powerful speech. He wore his body as casually as a cloak, and though it was a frail covering, less than a hundred pounds, the impression he gave was of immense stamina and strength, the measureless force of the spirit. In the gathering dusk the centuries seemed to roll away to reveal a glimpse of the Compassionate Buddha, giving the secret of nonviolence to a strife-torn world more than twenty-five hundred years before.

Scriptures from all religions, such as the Koran and the Sermon on the Mount, were recited at the prayer meetings. But it was always the Bhagavad Gita from which Gandhi drew his deepest inspiration and guidance. Mahadev Desai came and sat down near Gandhi and began to read the second chapter of the Gita, which describes the perfect man. All his life Gandhi had worked to translate these ideals into his daily life. As the sonorous verses came forth you could see him completely absorbed, his mind growing calm and still and his mighty spirit being released. His concentration was so complete that it was no longer the second chapter you were listening to, it was the second chapter you were seeing, witnessing for yourself the transformation it describes:

> They are forever free who have broken
> Out of the ego-cage of *I* and *mine*
> To be united with the Lord of Love.
> This is the supreme state. Attain thou this
> And pass from death to immortality.

"The art of dying follows as a corollary from the art of living."

It was on such an evening that the final tragedy was enacted. Gandhi was in Delhi, consuming every waking moment in a last plea for Hindu-Muslim unity. When it came time for the prayer meeting he walked to it briskly, as he always did, with his arms on the shoulders of two of the ashram girls. A dense crowd had gathered to hear him speak. As he walked to the platform through the crowd Gandhi held his palms together in front of him in greeting. And as he did so, a young man blinded by hatred placed himself in Gandhi's path, greeted him with the same gesture of his hands, and fired a gun point-blank into Gandhi's heart. Such is the greatness of this little man's love that as his body fell, nothing but the mantram which was deep within him came to his lips, *Rama, Rama, Rama.* It meant *I forgive you, I love you, I bless you.*

A human being is an immense spiritual force barely contained in a physical form. When all his hopes, all his desires, all his drive, all his will fuse together and become one, this force is released even in his own lifetime, and not even the death of his body can imprison it again. Gandhi made himself the force of nonviolence. He is a force which cannot die, which awakens again wherever a person or a community or a nation turns to nonviolence with all its strength and all its will.

Once, while Gandhi's train was pulling slowly out of the station, a reporter ran up to him and asked him breathlessly for a message to take back to his people. Gandhi's reply was a hurried line scrawled on a scrap of paper: "My life is my message." It is a message which does not require the vast stage of world politics, but can be put into practice here and now, in the midst of daily life.

On his evening walk.

"I have nothing new to teach the world. Truth and nonviolence are as old as the hills. All I have done is to try experiments in both on as vast a scale as I could do. In doing so, I have sometimes erred and learnt by my errors. Life and its problems have thus become to me so many experiments in the practice of truth and nonviolence. . . .

"Well, all my philosophy, if it may be called by that pretentious name, is contained in what I have said. But, you will not call it 'Gandhism'; there is no 'ism' about it. And no elaborate literature or propaganda is needed about it. The scriptures have been quoted against my position, but I have held faster than ever to the position that truth may not be sacrificed for anything whatsoever. Those who believe in the simple truths I have laid down can propagate them only by living them."

On his morning walk,

1944.

(Courtesy R.V. Pandit)

"*I have not the shadow of a doubt that any man or woman can achieve what I have, if he or she would make the same effort and cultivate the same hope and faith.*"

*With Khan Abdul
Ghaffar Khan on an
early morning walk in
Bihar, 1947.*

(Jagan V. Mehta)

145

How Nonviolence Works

BY TIMOTHY FLINDERS

In the preceding pages, Eknath Easwaran has stressed Gandhi's personal development as a spiritual figure and political innovator. Here I want to go deeper into the essentials of satyagraha, as Gandhi explained them, to see how this approach can be applied to contemporary problems.

We are used to thinking of satyagraha as a technique for social action, which Gandhi used to free India of British rule. This is true as far as it goes, but it falls short of Gandhi's intent. Satyagraha is actually a way to approach conflict and resolve it nonviolently, on many levels of human interaction. Its use begins with the individual and in the home and extends to the community, to institutions, and to countries. Wherever conflict arises, subtle or violent, satyagraha has a place of importance.

As Gandhi developed it, satyagraha is not simply a technique or theory, but a way of life. All of Gandhi's ideas bear this imprint, that they achieve their potential only in their application, "only by living them." Gandhi did not invent satyagraha, he discovered it; satyagraha, he said, is "as old as the hills." Gandhi defined its principles and applied them on as large a scale as possible to show their efficacy. But all the while he made it clear that the practice of satyagraha had to begin with the individual, "at home."

As he rode through the London streets with Gandhi to the 1931 Round Table Conference, G. D. Birla, one of Gandhi's millionaire supporters in India, wondered if Gandhi had prepared the speech he was to give that morning. "I suppose," Birla said, "you have thought of what you want to say."

"I am absolutely blank," Gandhi replied, "but perhaps God will help me in collecting my thoughts at the proper time. After all, we have to talk like simple men. I have no desire to appear extra intelligent. Like a simple villager, all that I have to say is: 'We want independence.'"

Gandhi developed satyagraha with "simple" people in mind, so that its power would be accessible to the average man and woman. Satyagraha requires no higher degrees or special training, since it is founded on the most fundamental law of human nature, love. We all have the capacity for satyagraha within us, Gandhi assured us, but we do not know how to release its "irresistible" power.

"I will give you a talisman. Whenever you are in doubt or when the self becomes too much with you, try the following expedient: Recall the face of the poorest and the most helpless man whom you may have seen and ask yourself if the step you contemplate is going to be of any use to him. Will he be able to gain anything by it? Will it restore him to a control over his own life and destiny? In other words, will it lead to . . . self-rule for the hungry and also spiritually starved millions of our countrymen? Then you will find your doubts and your self melting away."

Satyagraha means many things to different people, and Gandhi himself uses the term broadly. When reduced to its essentials, satyagraha is neither a movement for independence nor a technique of political action, though, in fact, it comes to mean these at different times. Satyagraha is, simply enough, a spiritual force – a potent, viable source of energy that belongs to all individuals, though few are aware of it.

In 1908, in South Africa, Gandhi deliberately coined the word *satyagraha*. He had a precise force in mind and sought equally precise language to define it, particularly to free it from association with the term "passive resistance." In his account of the South African struggle he defines satyagraha this way: "Truth (*satya*) implies love, and Firmness (*agraha*) engenders and therefore serves as a synonym for force. I thus began to call the Indian movement 'satyagraha'; that is to say, the force which is born of truth and love or nonviolence. . . ."

The word is self-defining, and clearly captures the substance of

Gandhi's idea, from its conception in South Africa at the turn of the century to the final clashes with the British Raj during World War II. During that time satyagraha assumed many forms – marches, hartals, fasts, boycotts, civil disobedience. But to Gandhi it always remained unmistakably a force, born of the search for truth and a firm adherence to nonviolence.

Satya, truth, means literally "that which is": that which never changes, but holds true at all times and under all circumstances. To Gandhi this was equivalent to God: "Truth is God," he declared, but added as a caution, "God alone knows absolute Truth." We, on the other hand, can pursue only a relative truth; but if our search for truth is pure and devoid of self-interest, Gandhi believed, we will not come to harm.

". . . what may appear as truth to one person will often appear as untruth to another person. But that need not worry the seeker. Where there is honest effort, it will be realized that what appear to be different truths are like the countless and apparently different leaves of the same tree. . . . Truth is the right designation of God. Hence there is nothing wrong in every man following Truth according to his lights. Indeed it is his duty to do so. Then if there is a mistake on the part of anyone so following Truth, it will be automatically set right. For the quest of Truth involves tapas – self-suffering, sometimes even unto death. There can be no place in it for even a trace of self-interest. In such selfless search for Truth nobody can lose his bearings for long."

The dictionary definition of *agraha* is "insisting on," "strong or obstinate inclination for," "obstinacy." Gandhi, it is clear, chose his terms with care; satyagraha was for him a firm, in fact, an obstinate clinging to truth, whatever the context. The "indomitable will" one brings to the quest – *that* lends it force.

But truth alone is not enough. Gandhi knew human nature and felt that, by itself, truth could become "unethical": "It is because we have at the present moment everybody claiming the right of conscience without going through any discipline whatsoever that there is so much untruth being delivered to a bewildered world." What can make the search for truth impure, "unethical," is his "self-interest." Gandhi's antidote to untruth was the systematic reduction of self-centeredness, which he spelled out in a simple tenet, "Reduce yourself to zero." This reduction of self-will is the discipline he mentions above, and without it, the search for truth can lead to self-righteousness, arrogance, even tyranny.

"There comes a time when an individual becomes irresistible and his action becomes all-pervasive in its effects. This comes when he reduces himself to zero."

Self-will blocks the release of the tremendous inner power of satyagraha; removing self-will frees it. This power may be compared to the genius that artists refer to when they say, "I got myself out of the way." Gandhi called it "soul-force": "Satyagraha," he says, "is soul-force pure and simple."

Gandhi does not mean to be metaphorical here; he meant *force.* He believed, and his life demonstrated, that under certain conditions all men and women have a tremendous power available to them, and their "action becomes all-pervasive in its effects." They become "irresistible," not overcoming opposition with force but melting it away, finally with its own consent. To name this force "passive resistance" betrays an ignorance of its active power. It would be as much to call light "non-darkness," which implies wrongly that light is the absence of something else and obscures the fact that light is a form of energy, which, when properly understood, can illuminate cities. Similarly with satyagraha. There is a tremendous power here, obscured by ignorance and language, which Gandhi would say can solve the most difficult of human problems when properly understood. As light achieves great power when it is intensified in the laser, the power of the individual becomes irresistible through self-discipline, "when he reduces himself to zero." Gandhi tried to show through his own life that the human being who is devoid of self-interest is the instrument which reveals this energy and puts it to work to resolve conflict at any level. But he made it clear that this power is not confined to a select few, but is potentially available to all:

"[*Satyagraha*] *is a force that may be used by individuals as well as by communities. It may be used as well in political as in domestic affairs. Its universal applicability is a demonstration of its permanence and invincibility. It can be used alike by men, women, and children.*"

Ahimsa

Ahimsa, nonviolence, was the noblest expression of Truth for Gandhi – or, properly speaking, the way to truth.

"*Ahimsa and Truth are so intertwined that it is practically impossible to disentangle and separate them. They are like the two sides of a coin, or rather a smooth unstamped metallic disc. Who can say which is the obverse and which the reverse? Nevertheless, ahimsa is the means; Truth is the end.*"

Ahimsa is the bedrock of satyagraha, the "irreducible minimum" to which satyagraha adheres and the final measure of its value. In the traditional lore of India there is a story about an old sannyasi, a Hindu monk, who was sitting on the bank of a river silently repeating his mantram. Nearby a scorpion fell from a tree into the river, and the sannyasi, seeing it struggling in the water, bent over and pulled it out. He placed the scorpion back in the tree, but as he did so, the creature bit him on the hand. He paid no heed to the bite, but went on repeating his mantram. A little while later, the scorpion again fell into the water. As before, the monk pulled him out and set him back in the tree and again was bitten. This little drama was repeated several times, and each time the sannyasi rescued the scorpion, he received a bite.

It happened that a villager, ignorant of the ways of holy men, had come to the river for water and had seen the whole affair. Unable to contain himself any longer, the villager told the sannyasi with some vexation:

"Swamiji, I have seen you save that foolish scorpion several times now and each time he has bitten you. Why not let the rascal go?"

"Brother," replied the sannyasi, "the fellow cannot help himself. It is his nature to bite."

"Agreed," answered the villager. "But knowing this, why don't you avoid him?"

"Ah, brother," replied the monk, "you see, I cannot help myself either. I am a human being; it is my nature to save."

Ahimsa is usually translated as "nonviolence," but as we have seen, its meaning goes much beyond that. *Ahimsa* is derived from the Sanskrit verb root *han,* which means to kill. The form *hims* means "desirous to kill," the prefix *a-* is a negation. So *a-himsa* means literally "lacking any desire to kill," which is perhaps the central theme upon which Hindu, Jain, and Buddhist morality is built. In the *Manu Smriti,* the great law book of Hinduism, it is written, "*Ahimsa paramo dharma*": ahimsa is the highest law. It is, as Gandhi puts it, the very essence of human nature.

"Nonviolence is the law of our species as violence is the law of the brute. The spirit lies dormant in the brute and he knows no law but that of physical might. The dignity of man requires obedience to a higher law — to the strength of the spirit. . . ."

The word *nonviolence* connotes a negative, almost passive condition, whereas the Sanskrit term *ahimsa* suggests a dynamic state of mind in which power is released. "Strength," Gandhi said, "does not come from physical capacity. It comes from an indomitable will." Therein he found his own strength, and there he exhorted others to look for theirs. Latent in the depths of human consciousness, this inner strength can be cultivated by the observance of complete ahimsa. Whereas violence checks this energy within, and is ultimately disruptive in its consequences, ahimsa, properly understood, is invincible. "With satya combined with ahimsa," Gandhi writes, "you can bring the world to your feet."

When Gandhi speaks of ahimsa as a law, we should take him at his word. Indeed, it was a law for him like gravity, and could be demonstrated in the midst of human affairs. Gandhi even characterized his practice of ahimsa as a science, and said once, "I have been practicing with scientific precision nonviolence and its possibilities for an unbroken period of over fifty years." He was a precise man, meticulous and exacting, fond of quoting a Marathi hymn that goes, "Give me love, give me peace, O Lord, but don't deny me common sense." He valued experience as the test of truth, and the nonviolence he pursued and called "true nonviolence" had to conform to experience in all levels of human affairs. "I have applied it," he declares, "in every walk of life: domestic, institutional, economic, political. And I know of no single case in which it has failed." Anything short of this total application did not interest Gandhi, because ahimsa sprang from and worked in the same continuum as his religion, politics, and personal life. Only practice could determine its value, "when it acts in the midst of and in spite of opposition," and he advised critics to observe the results of his experiments rather than dissect his theories.

"... nonviolence is not a cloistered virtue to be practiced by the individual for his peace and final salvation, but it is a rule of conduct for society. ... To practice nonviolence in mundane matters is to know its true value. It is to bring heaven upon earth. ... I hold it therefore to be wrong to limit the use of nonviolence to cave dwellers [hermits] and for acquiring merit for a favoured position in the other world. All virtue ceases to have use if it serves no purpose in every walk of life."

Gandhi's adherence to nonviolence grew from his experience that it was the only way to resolve the problem of conflict permanently. Violence, he felt, only made the pretense of a solution, and sowed seeds of bitterness and enmity that would ultimately disrupt the situation.

One needs to practice ahimsa to understand it. To profess nonviolence with sincerity or even to write a book about it was, for Gandhi, not adequate. "If one does not practice nonviolence in one's personal relationships with others one is vastly mistaken. Nonviolence, like charity, must begin at home." The practice of nonviolence is by no means a simple matter, and Gandhi never intimated that it was. As a discipline, a "code of conduct," true nonviolence demands endless vigilance over one's entire way of life, because it includes words and thought as well as actions.

"Ahimsa is not the crude thing it has been made to appear. Not to hurt any living thing is no doubt a part of ahimsa. But it is its least expression. The principle of ahimsa is hurt by every evil thought, by undue haste, by lying, by hatred, by wishing ill to anybody. It is also violated by our holding on to what the world needs."

It can readily be seen that the practice of ahimsa is a serious matter. Lived properly, it would alter the fabric of life. True ahimsa might require a lifetime to learn, but Gandhi is not talking about a momentary diversion or pastime. He is talking about changing the face of the world, and he is quite serious.

"Nonviolence in its dynamic condition means conscious suffering. It does not mean meek submission to the will of the evil-doer, but it means pitting of one's whole soul against the will of the tyrant. Working under this law of our being, it is possible for a single individual to defy the whole might of an unjust empire to save his honor, his religion, his soul, and lay the foundation for that empire's fall or its regeneration."

Ahimsa is not meek. This is a common misconception. Ahimsa faces the opponent with kindness and sympathy but with the sure determination that whatever the opposition, it will hold its ground. Unlike violence, ahimsa is subtle and pervasive, so that we are not likely to be aware of its work. Its subtlety does not diminish its efficacy; on the contrary, it makes it more difficult to oppose:

"Nonviolence is like radium in its action. An infinitesimal quantity of it embedded in a malignant growth acts continuously, silently, and ceaselessly till it has transformed the whole mass of the diseased tissue into a healthy one. Similarly, even a little of true nonviolence acts in a silent, subtle, unseen way and leavens the whole society."

Satya-graha

"South Africa is a representative of Western civilization while India is the centre of Oriental culture. Thinkers of the present generation hold that these two civilizations cannot go together. If nations representing these rival cultures meet even in small groups, the result will only be an explosion. The West is opposed to simplicity while Orientals consider that virtue to be of primary importance. How can these opposite views be reconciled? ...

"Western civilization may or may not be good, but Westerners wish to stick to it. They have shed rivers of blood for its sake. It is therefore too late for them now to chalk out a new path for themselves. Thus considered, the Indian question cannot be resolved into one of trade jealousy or race hatred. The problem is simply one of preserving one's own civilization. ...

"The Indians are disliked in South Africa for their simplicity, patience, perseverance, frugality, and otherworldliness. Westerners are enterprising, impatient, engrossed in multiplying their material wants and in satisfying them, fond of good cheer, anxious to save physical labor and prodigal in habits. They are therefore afraid that if thousands of Orientals settled in South Africa, the Westerners must go to the wall. Westerners in South Africa are not prepared to commit suicide and their leaders will not permit them to be reduced to such straits."

Satyagraha, in practice, is a method for resolving conflict. Traditionally, conflict between opposed parties is "resolved" only by the acknowledged dominance of one antagonist over the other. The assumption is that one side can succeed only at the expense of the other. Success may come by reason or persuasion, by threat or blackmail, or by force, but in any case the assumption is the same: if there is to be a winner, there must be a loser. Even compromise rests on this assumption, since in a compromise one side attempts to get as much as it can at the expense of the other, compromising only to the extent it is forced by circumstances to do so.

Satyagraha challenges this assumption. Rather than trying to conquer the opponent or to annihilate his claims, satyagraha tries to resolve the sources of conflict. As Gandhi states succinctly, it "seeks to liquidate antagonisms but not the antagonists themselves." This

155

point is critical, since it quickly distinguishes satyagraha from other social action methods which merely attempt to gain self-invested ends. The purpose of satyagraha is not the redress of grievances; these are incidental to its ultimate aim, which is to resolve the underlying sources of conflict, the enmity, the distrust. Satyagraha seeks to resolve conflict by persuading the adversary of the common value of its nonviolent vision that he – we – have much more to gain in harmony than in discord. Bringing about this conversion in an opponent is always a primary aim of satyagraha, even though its actual methods may vary with circumstances.

Satyagraha does not, like violence, try to exclude the adversary from the solution. On the contrary, it tries to transform the opponent, drawing him in as a participant and beneficiary in the solution, and "aims to exalt both sides." Satyagraha does not view the adversary as an enemy to be overcome, but as a participant in the search for a truthful solution to the conflict. Rather than annihilate him, satyagraha tries to win him over to the side of truth, "to wean him from his error."

"This is in essence the principle of nonviolent noncooperation. It follows therefore that it must have its root in love. Its object should not be to punish the opponent or to inflict injury upon him. Even while noncooperating with him, we must make him feel that in us he has a friend and we should try to reach his heart by rendering him humanitarian service wherever possible."

"The basic principle on which the practice of nonviolence rests is that what holds good in respect of oneself equally applies to the whole universe. All mankind in essence are alike. What is therefore possible for me, is possible for everybody."

Satyagraha offers a new vision of truth and nonviolence. Gandhi's confidence that an opponent could be eventually won over to this vision lay in his belief that all men are invested with the same urge to find Truth, that "we are all tarred with the same brush." Since he sees himself and his opponent as embodying the same truth, the satyagrahi believes implicitly that through his response to "infinite patience and sympathy," the adversary will respond to this vision. The satyagrahi attempts to alter the relationship of conflict to one of esteem and trust, and he acts to purify it of distrust and ill will. This transformation is not had merely for the asking. The satyagrahi uses trust, support, sympathy – and, if necessary, his readiness to suffer – to gradually open up the heart of the adversary and disarm his opposition.

"We thus reached a provisional agreement after eight years of struggle and satyagraha was suspended for the last time. It was rather difficult to get the Indians to endorse this agreement. No one would wish that enthusiasm which had arisen should be allowed to subside. Again, whoever would trust General Smuts? Someone reminded me of the fiasco in 1908 and said, 'General Smuts once played us false, often charged you with forcing fresh issues, and subjected the community to endless suffering. And yet what a pity that you have not learnt the necessary lesson of declining to trust him! This man will betray you once again, and you will again propose to revive satyagraha. But who will then listen to you?'...

   "I knew that such arguments would be brought forward, and was not therefore surprised when they were. No matter how often a satyagrahi is betrayed, he will repose his trust in the adversary so long as there are not cogent grounds for distrust. Pain to a satyagrahi is the same as pleasure. He will not therefore be misled by the mere fear of suffering into groundless distrust. On the other hand, relying as he does upon his own strength, he will not mind being betrayed by the adversary, will continue to trust in spite of frequent betrayals, and will believe that he thereby strengthens the forces of truth and brings victory nearer. . . . Distrust is a sign of weakness and satyagraha implies the banishment of all weakness and therefore of distrust, which is clearly out of place when the adversary is not to be destroyed but to be won over."

In his attempt to win over the opponent, the satyagrahi tries to cooperate with him in whatever ways possible in order to build confidence

157

and respect. This process is essential to satyagraha, for upon this trust is built the edifice to which both parties will eventually turn in search of a resolution to their conflicts. The actual terms of the resolution are not, in fact, the main concern of satyagraha; rather it tries to establish a relationship of trust in which new terms can be arrived at. Thus it seeks first and always cooperation:

"Although noncooperation is one of the main weapons in the armory of satyagraha, it should not be forgotten that it is, after all, only a means to secure the cooperation of the opponent consistently with truth and justice. . . . Avoidance of all relationship with the opposing power, therefore, can never be a satyagrahi's object, but transformation or purification of that relationship."

If satyagraha's chief object is to persuade its adversary of its vision, where do methods like civil disobedience, strike, and noncooperation apply? Gandhi argued that when the appeal to reason fails, these methods provide the satyagrahi with the opportunity to suffer, which is the final and purest weapon the satyagrahi has with which to secure his vision.

"Meanwhile, we passed a few happy days in Volksrust jail, where new prisoners came every day and brought us news of what was happening outside. Among these Satyagrahi prisoners there was one old man named Harbatsinh who was about 75 years of age. Harbatsinh was not working on the mines which the Indians had struck. He had completed his indenture years ago and he was not therefore a striker. The Indians grew far more enthusiastic after my arrest, and many of them got arrested by crossing over from Natal into the Transvaal. Harbatsinh was one of these enthusiasts.

"'Why are you in jail?' I asked Harbatsinh. 'I have not invited old men like yourself to court jail.'

"'How could I help it,' replied Harbatsinh, 'when you, your wife, and even your boys went to jail for our sake?'

"'But you will not be able to endure the hardships of jail life. I would advise you to leave jail. Shall I arrange for your release?'

"'No, please. I will never leave jail. I must die one of these days, and how happy should I be to die in jail!'

"It was not for me to try to shake such determination, which would not have been shaken even if I had tried. My head bent in reverence before this illiterate sage. Harbatsinh had his wish and he died in Durban jail on January 5, 1914."

Gandhi's theory of satyagraha was drawn directly from his experiences in South Africa, and though ideal in nature, it was practical to the extreme in application. He lived by reason, but he knew that reason does not move men's hearts. Satyagraha, since it seeks to actually transform its adversaries, must appeal ultimately to the heart. Nevertheless, Gandhi always appealed first to the minds of his adversaries, and in all his campaigns one can observe an almost endless parade of appeals and petitions, delegations, conferences, resolutions, and exhortations. "Due process" is the first step in the process of satyagraha, but the ways of custom, law, and vested interest are often impervious to reason. Or, as is often the case in a conflict, what may be truth for one party is taken to be error by the other. Such an impasse usually marks the boiling point in conflict situations.

"In the application of satyagraha, I discovered, in the earliest stages, that pursuit of Truth did not admit of violence being inflicted on one's opponent, but that he must be weaned from error by patience and sympathy. For what appears to be truth to the one may appear to be error to the other. And patience means self-suffering. So the doctrine came to mean vindication of Truth, not by infliction of suffering on the opponent but one's own self."

When all attempts to reason have been made and the adversary remains unmoved, for whatever reason, there are usually two alternatives: find a way to change his heart or force him to revoke his claims. Traditional methods take the latter path and resort to violence, physical or subtle. The satyagrahi moves to melt the opponent's resistance and alter his perspective by inflicting suffering not on the opponent but on himself.

"Up to the year 1906 I simply relied on appeal to reason. I was a very industrious reformer. . . . But I found that reason failed to produce an impression when the critical moment arrived in South Africa. My people were excited; even a worm will and does some times turn – and there was talk of wreaking vengeance. I had then to choose between allying myself to violence or finding out some other method of meeting the crisis and stopping the rot; and it came to me that we should refuse to obey the legislation that was degrading and let them put us in jail if they liked. Thus came into being the moral equivalent of war. . . . Since then the conviction has been growing upon me, that things of fundamental importance to the people are not secured by reason alone but have to be purchased with their suffering. Suffering is the law of human beings; war is the law of the jungle. But suffering is infinitely more powerful than the law of the jungle for converting the opponent and opening his ears, which are otherwise shut, to the voice of reason. . . . I have come to this fundamental conclusion, that if you want something really important to be done you must not merely satisfy the reason, you must move the heart also. The appeal to reason is more to the head but the penetration of the heart comes from suffering. It opens up the inner understanding in man."

Thus self-suffering became the hallmark of satyagraha, the ultimate weapon to move men's hearts. Civil disobedience, strikes, and noncooperation were all methods designed not to coerce the South Africans – or, later, the British – but to soften their hearts by the visible suffering they wrought upon the satyagrahis. The immediate fruits of civil disobedience were jail, dispossession, physical injury, and sometimes even death. Gandhi made this point emphatically, yet it is often overlooked: "Satyagraha and its offshoots, noncooperation and passive resistance, are nothing but new names for the law of suffering."

In his effort to build trust, the satyagrahi must be careful not to harass or embarrass his opponent and will go out of his way to afford him every courtesy. To the casual observer of Gandhi's satyagraha campaigns, it might appear that he followed this even at the expense of his own cause. But change is not easy, and in political conflict, satyagraha may demand breaks from tradition and custom. The satyagrahi knows that the transformation he asks from his opponent will be difficult, so he tries to be aware of any hardships he may cause his adversary and to ease those hardships wherever he can. His object is not to attack or harass persons but to change systems that obstruct the public welfare.

SOUTH AFRICA
Natal, 1913

"When the Indian labourers on the north coast went on strike, the planters at Mount Edgecombe would have been put to great losses if all the cane that had been cut was not brought to the mill and crushed. Twelve hundred Indians therefore returned to work solely with a view to finish this part of the work, and joined their compatriots only when it was finished. Again when the Indian employees of the Durban Municipality struck work, those who were engaged in the sanitary services of the borough or as attendants upon the patients in hospitals were sent back, and they willingly returned to their duties. If the sanitary services were dislocated, and if there was no one to attend upon the patients in hospitals, there might be an outbreak of disease in the city and the sick would be deprived of medical aid, and no satyagrahi would wish for such consequences to ensue. Employees of this description were therefore exempted from the strike. In every step that he takes, the satyagrahi is bound to consider the position of his adversary. I could see that the numerous cases of such chivalry left their invisible yet potent impress everywhere . . . and prepared a suitable atmosphere for a settlement."

His sympathy, his patience, his trust, and his willingness to suffer are the main "weapons" with which the satyagrahi transforms his opponent and alters the nature of the conflict relationship. From mistrust and enmity, the relationship evolves to trust, respect, and cooperation. When this is reached, Gandhi holds, the points of conflict and tension will be amicably resolved, since the "adversary" is now, in a sense, an ally, and sees the promise that a cooperative solution holds for both parties. He understands that there is something at stake much higher than his private vested interests and is moved to subordinate them to that promise. In a way the adversary shares in the

161

vision of satyagraha and – it would not be too much to say – becomes something of a satyagrahi himself. This "conversion" of the opponent is the real intent of satyagraha, and its use of strikes, demonstrations, and the like are merely tools to bring it about.

"It is the acid test of nonviolence that in a nonviolent conflict there is no rancor left behind and, in the end, the enemies are converted into friends. That was my experience in South Africa with General Smuts. He started with being my bitterest opponent and critic. Today he is my warmest friend. . . . "

The vision to which satyagraha attempts to persuade its opponents goes beyond the particular grievances in a given struggle, such as discriminating legislation or unjust taxes. These are usually symptoms of a greater injustice or "untruth," whose amelioration is satyagraha's real aim. As such, a satyagraha campaign is never committed inflexibly to oppose any particular grievances; in this regard it is open-ended. Having declared its irreducible minimum – a firm adherence to truth and nonviolence – satyagraha is free to adapt to the dynamics of the struggle. This open-endedness lends satyagraha a kind of tensile strength which makes it possible to change a position whenever the truth of a situation appears in a new light due to altered circumstances. Gandhi calls this the "law of progression":

"My experience has taught me that a law of progression applies to every righteous struggle. But in the case of satyagraha, the law amounts to an axiom. As a satyagraha struggle progresses onward, many another element helps to swell its current and there is a constant growth in the results to which it leads. This is really inevitable and is bound up with the first principles of satyagraha. For in satyagraha, the minimum is also the maximum; and as it is the irreducible minimum, there is no question of retreat and the only possible movement is an advance."

Open-endedness encourages the satyagrahi to look continually for truth in a campaign, even in his opponent's position, and to incorporate that truth into his own position. This marks a critical step, for the mere disposition to reconsider one's position can neutralize the atmosphere of conflict, making it less rigid and creating a climate in which there can be give-and-take. Within this climate of trust, antagonistic claims can evolve into a synthesized, unified expression of truth. This process is the practical expression of satyagraha's unitary vision: that, in fact, we are all seekers after the same truth. Therefore Gandhi will exhort, "A satyagrahi never misses a chance of compromise on honorable terms...." Satyagraha's unitary vision springs from the depths of human need and is thus compelling. In its revealing light, petty antagonisms and grievances give way to the more promising search for harmony.

SOUTH
AFRICA
The Transvaal,
1914

"I went to Pretoria with Andrews. Just at this time there was a great strike of the European employees of the Union railways, which made the position of the government extremely delicate. I was called upon to commence the Indian march against the government at such a fortunate juncture. But I declared that the Indians could not assist the railway strikers, as they were not out to harass the government, their struggle being entirely different and differently conceived. Even if we undertook the march, we would begin it at some other time when the railway trouble had ended. This decision of ours created a deep impression, and was cabled to England by Reuter. Lord Ampthill [Secretary of the Colonies] cabled his congratulations from England. English friends in South Africa too appreciated our decision."

Success in satyagraha never depends upon the acceptance of particular terms, but is measured solely by the purity of its cause and the firmness with which it adheres to truth and nonviolence. For Gandhi, a pure end could be achieved only when the means were pure; he saw "the same inviolable connection between the means and the end as there is between the seed and the tree." He urges the satyagrahi to look constantly at his effort, because "full effort is full victory." When the means are pure, the end will take care of itself; if the means are despoiled by untruth or violence, the end will likewise be despoiled. For Gandhi, this was common sense:

"Nevertheless ahimsa is the means; Truth is the end. Means, to be means, must be always within our reach, and so ahimsa is our supreme duty. If we take care of the means, we are bound to reach the end sooner or later. When once we have grasped this point, final victory is beyond question. Whatever difficulties we encounter, whatever apparent reverse we sustain, we may not give up the quest for Truth. . . ."

In violent conflict, bitterness and enmity accompany conquest and can fester like boils, undermining the achievement, or explode, reversing it. The conquest of satyagraha is permanent because no one is conquered. In true satyagraha both parties emerge as partners in the solution; only the conflict, enmity, and distrust are purged. One need only watch the film footage of Imperial British troops leaving India in 1947, cheering and being cheered, to suspect this truth. As Arnold Toynbee remarked at the time, Gandhi had not only liberated India, he had also liberated Great Britain.

"One of General Smuts' secretaries said jocularly to me: 'I do not like your people, and do not care to assist them at all. But what am I to do? You help us in our days of need. How can we lay hands upon you? I often wish you took to violence like the English strikers, and then we would know at once how to dispose of you. But you will not injure even the enemy. You desire victory by self-imposed limits of courtesy and chivalry. And that is what reduces us to sheer helplessness.'"

Satya-graha Today

Up to now we have looked at the way satyagraha works in the political sphere, but the principles that guide satyagraha apply equally in personal, domestic, and community affairs. The purpose of satyagraha is to resolve underlying sources of conflict – any conflict – and bring adversaries into a field of mutual understanding and cooperation. For Gandhi it did not matter if the adversaries were the Indian Congress and the British Raj, a group of peasants and their landlord, or a husband and wife; satyagraha may be used, he said, "by individuals as well as by communities. It may be used as well in political as in domestic affairs. Its universal applicability is a demonstration of its permanence and invincibility."

Clearly, Gandhi had something in mind that goes far beyond the exclusive political applications with which we identify satyagraha today. He assigned it a fundamental position in human affairs and considered it a comprehensive solution to human conflict. To understand satyagraha in the full Gandhian sense, we need to move away from the current view that sees satyagraha only as a form of mass, nonviolent protest, and try to understand it in its more personal ramifications. In this way satyagraha's usefulness to our own lives will be more evident

"SELF-SATYAGRAHA"

Satyagraha is not a "method," strictly speaking, any more than love is a method. Gandhi saw satyagraha as essentially an attitude, an interior condition of nonviolent love which frames our relationship with the rest of humanity. This attitude comes from within, not without. As Gandhi conceived it, satyagraha is first and last a personal matter: "I have always maintained," he wrote, "that even if there is one individual who is almost completely nonviolent, he can put out the conflagration." Gandhi so believed in the essential *individualness* of satyagraha that he would finally say, "If a single satyagrahi holds out to the end, victory is certain." Far from a doctrine of mass action, satyagraha is fundamentally a private affair that begins within the human heart, and requires no followers to make itself felt. Its power is independent of number; satyagraha is portable, like a small but powerful lamp that can be trained on any corner of life darkened by conflict or tension. "That is the beauty of satyagraha," Gandhi wrote. "It comes up to oneself; one has not to go out in search for it." It needs only to be anchored firmly within the heart. This is the first requisite of Gandhi's satyagraha, and the more clearly we understand this, the sooner we can use satyagraha to heal the wounds of conflict.

Simply understanding this, however, is not sufficient. As we have seen, satyagraha grows out of discipline aimed at the removal of self-interest. Gandhi was adamant in this regard: "Without self-purification," he wrote, "the observance of the law of ahimsa must remain an empty dream." An individual can generate the "irresistible" power of satyagraha only when he has become "passion-free in thought, speech and action," able "to rise above the opposing currents of love and hatred, attachment and repulsion." Stripped of its disciplines, satyagraha is without its fundamental source of strength, that "soul-force" by which alone it commands our attention. The person who studies Gandhi to learn the source of nonviolent power will repeatedly be turned back upon himself and urged to establish nonviolence in his own consciousness. "There is no royal road," Gandhi wrote in the late thirties, "except through living the creed in your life, which must be a living sermon. Of course, the expression in one's own life presupposes great study, tremendous perseverance, and thorough cleansing of oneself...." But why worry if it takes a long time to master, he added, "for, if this is the only permanent thing in life, if this is the only thing that counts, then whatever effort you bestow on mastering it is well spent. 'Seek ye first the kingdom of heaven and everything else shall be added unto you.' The kingdom of heaven is ahimsa."

This is a tall order. What Gandhi asks amounts to a kind of "self-satyagraha" that the individual imposes upon himself or herself to neutralize self-interest. Gandhi can make the demand because, characteristically, he did just that himself. The long night in the empty train station at Maritzburg forced Gandhi to look beyond himself for the first time, beyond his private needs and into the heart of the terrible suffering of his impoverished and exploited countrymen. The vision that haunted him during those lonely, solemn hours waiting for dawn changed him, changed his way of looking at life and its purpose. Gandhi will speak of a number of inspirations in his life – Tolstoy and Ruskin, those long, forced walks during the Zulu rebellion, the dream in Madras that suggested his epic Salt March – but his experience on that cold night in Maritzburg proved to be the catalyst that set into motion a long series of experiments which, in time, transformed him utterly. The South African satyagraha lay more than a decade ahead, and the notion of satyagraha was still in Gandhi's future, unnamed, unthought-of. Yet those years of intense striving in which Gandhi confronted and uprooted his own self-interest mark for him that same purifying self-satyagraha he asks of us. In this sense, Gandhi's first opponent in nonviolent resistance was not General Smuts or the South African government, but Mohandas Gandhi; and the setting of his first and fiercest nonviolent campaign was his own consciousness. That struggle fashioned the first satyagrahi, and out of it the "briefless barrister" emerged the "mahatma," the great soul. To trace the real source of Gandhi's nonviolent power, we need to look beyond the period of political upheaval in India with which the world is familiar, to those quiet, formative years in the countryside of Natal and the Transvaal. It is there that Gandhi experimented with and found the path that would transfigure that simple, uncertain lawyer, and it is there that we can best find, for our own enlightenment, the sources of that transformation.

But we would do Gandhi an injustice to take him literally and merely imitate him on a superficial level. To shave our heads or wear a cotton dhoti, to live on fruits, nuts, and goat's milk because Gandhi did, misses the point. We should be cautious in following Gandhi to be sure that we get hold of basic principles and not merely the symbols by which he communicated his message. Patience, sympathy, and the willingness to endure are the fundamental criteria for self-satyagraha, just as they are for political satyagraha. Ordering our lives in conformity to those ideals – as Gandhi ordered his life – constitutes the first step along the path to true and lasting nonviolence.

FAMILY SATYAGRAHA

Personal relationships offer fertile ground to learn and use satyagraha. Gandhi called this "domestic satyagraha." We get a clear idea of what he meant when we look at his early life in South Africa – not, interestingly enough, at satyagraha as he was to develop it later, but as it was used against him. Gandhi was a domineering, sometimes petulant husband during those years in Johannesburg, because he believed, as he recounts, that it was his right to impose his will upon his wife. When Kasturbai objected to his unilateral approach, Gandhi only became more adamant. But Kasturbai had an intuitive grasp of the properties of nonviolent love, and during those tumultuous years of domestic strife, she proved to be Gandhi's equal. Her attitude transformed his relationship with her and in the process revealed to him the beauty and the power of nonviolent resistance.

"I learnt the lesson of nonviolence from my wife, when I tried to bend her to my will. Her determined resistance to my will, on the one hand, and her quiet submission to the suffering my stupidity involved, on the other, ultimately made me ashamed of myself and cured me of my stupidity . . . in the end, she became my teacher in nonviolence."

Without knowing it, Kasturbai had used satyagraha's foremost weapons to win over her husband: a readiness to suffer rather than retaliate, and an implacable will.

Family satyagraha is founded, like all satyagraha, on this delicate balance of patience and determination, which, when rightly practiced, can become a cornerstone for deep personal relations between men and women. The discovery Gandhi made in his own household at the turn of the century in Johannesburg is of critical importance today, when these relationships have become fraught with competition and tension. Few homes today seem able to withstand even the predictable tensions of married life, so that estrangement and alienation have become common ingredients in the modern household. At this low ebb in family living, Gandhi's way rings especially true: forgive, forbear, support the other person always, and when it becomes necessary to resist, do so lovingly and without rancor. The apex of this ideal is reached when the wife's welfare becomes more important to the husband than his own happiness, and the husband's welfare takes on a similar importance to the wife. This kind of relationship marks one of the highest achievements of true ahimsa.

Between parents and children, satyagraha has a natural place. Here again, patience mingled with firmness frames the approach. The "irreducible minimum" in family satyagraha is that the welfare of the children comes first; their growth and development take precedence over everything else. It means making minor sacrifices of small pleasures at times or saying no, gently but firmly, more often than one wants to. Most important, in Gandhi's thinking, is that the example set by the parents be true to their ideals. When Gandhi moved to Tolstoy Farm in 1909, it was with a motley group of children whom he immediately took under his fatherly wing. They were an "ill-assorted" lot, but in Gandhi's eyes, he and they were "all one family." "I saw," he writes, "that I must be good and live straight, if only for their sakes." The seeds of family satyagraha were sown by Gandhi in the rich soil of Tolstoy Farm, and years of careful husbandry brought them into full bloom; in time, this demanding relationship with children became a natural, almost effortless attitude for him.

During the thirties a woman came to Sevagram asking Gandhi to get her little boy to stop eating sugar; it was doing him harm. Gandhi gave a cryptic reply: "Please come back next week."

The woman left puzzled but returned a week later, dutifully following the Mahatma's instructions. "Please don't eat sugar," Gandhi told the young fellow when he saw him. "It is not good for you." Then he joked with the boy for a while, gave him a hug, and sent him on his way. But the mother, unable to contain her curiosity, lingered behind to ask, "Bapu, why didn't you say this last week when we came? Why did you make us come back again?"

Gandhi smiled. "Last week," he said to her, "I too was eating sugar."

Gandhi was personal in all his relations. Even at the height of the freedom movement in India, he would not allow his campaigns to drift into nonpersonal postures. Regardless of how institutional his opponents might appear behind their marbled corridors and initialed titles, Gandhi's adversaries were always people first, "tarred with the same brush" and akin to him in their common humanity. Personal relationships were neither a luxury nor an imposition to Gandhi, but rather a natural and vital expression of ahimsa; at each level of human interaction they build the forum in which satyagraha operates. It is interesting to watch Gandhi's circle of friendships gradually evolve from his immediate family in Porbandar and Johannesburg to his many followers living in his ashrams, until finally it included all India and much of the world.

SATYAGRAHA AT WORK

One natural consequence of personalized satyagraha is its easy application in our place of work. What is true of family relationships is at least partly true of relationships at work, and if these relationships are less emotionally encumbered than those at home, they can be equally disruptive. Work never stops, and wherever people work closely together, tension is likely simply because of conflicting self-interest. As long as individuals in a working environment give their own self-interest highest priority, friction is unavoidable. The conflicts that result often center around personal opinions and tastes, differing ways of doing things; and they are frequently fueled by petty jealousies and resentments. The "issues" in most conflicts may appear professional, even philosophic, but a closer look often uncovers two unbending egos locked in personal combat. The "best" way of doing things is usually "my" way; as an Indian sage once put it simply, "Everyone thinks his watch has the right time."

In the satyagraha of work, an effort is made to clear the situation of personal preferences so that both parties can see the larger and truer perspective. The satyagrahi who has risen above self-interest, who can see beyond his own opinions, is in a position to view conflict with some objectivity and therefore able to look for common ground. If reasoned appeals fail, he must be prepared, as in all satyagraha, to forbear and win the parties over to the higher view. So the task of satyagraha here is to work silently and steadily to minimize self-interest in the working environment through the appeal to a broader, unifying purpose. Only one individual is necessary to spread the leavening influence of ahimsa in an office, a business, a school, or even a large institution; one dedicated satyagrahi, as Gandhi pointed out, can alter the climate so that work can proceed in an atmosphere of mutual trust and cooperation. This, Gandhi would say, echoing the Buddha, is the highest kind of work.

One of the main features of satyagraha, as we have seen, is its "open-endedness," its capacity to adapt creatively to new contexts while adhering to its irreducible principles of truth and nonviolence. This flexibility has never been more important than today, when the challenges we face are so different from those Gandhi confronted. Merely to imitate the forms of Gandhi's political campaigns, such as strikes and demonstrations, would tragically limit satyagraha to the narrow context of political reform. The crises that threaten our lives today are not so much political as spiritual: personal and social matters of alienation, isolation, and increasing polarization between men and women, old and young. Consequently, our times require a determined movement towards nonviolence and unity in our families and communities.

When the lives of millions of individuals are grounded in the values of nonviolence, Gandhi believed, larger institutions will begin to reflect these values as well. The path he charts begins in miniature, at home, within each individual and amidst relations and friends and gradually widens its arc to embrace the community, the society, and in time perhaps the world. We need no further proof of this than Gandhi's own life, which even today reaches us across half a century with its silent but quickening call to greater love and greater service.

More About Gandhi & Ahimsa

This list is divided into two parts: books which enable the reader to learn more about Gandhi the man and his ideas, and books that are helpful for those who wish to translate some of Gandhi's ideals into their own lives in the West today.

GANDHI THE MAN

Gandhi was a voluminous writer, and there are many good collections of material from his newspaper articles, editorials, letters, and speeches. Most of the quotations in this book can be found in two of the most comprehensive of these collections: *The Mind of Mahatma Gandhi,* edited by R. K. Prabhu and U. R. Rao (Ahmedabad: Navajivan Publishing House, 1960) and *All Men Are Brothers,* edited by Krishna Kripalani (New York: Columbia University Press, 1958). Both these books present Gandhi's thoughts on every aspect of his life, work, and faith.

Gandhi was the author of only two full-length books, both written in jail. *An Autobiography: The Story of My Experiments with Truth* (Boston: Beacon Press, 1957) is in print in the United States; but it is highly personal and inclined to be self-critical. Also, its narrative goes only as far as 1921, and since it is concerned primarily with Gandhi's spiritual development rather than his public political activity, and consequently assumes so much that is unfamiliar to Western readers, a good biography is essential for filling in the background. *Gandhi: His Life and Message for the World,* by Louis Fischer (New York: New American Library, Signet Books, 1954), serves this purpose; Fischer knew Gandhi personally, and brought to his book a sensitivity to the spiritual basis of Gandhi's life and to Gandhi the man. For those who want a more detailed account of Gandhi's life and the historical background of the movement for India's independence, *The Life of Mahatma Gandhi* (New York: Macmillan, Collier Books, 1962), is Fischer's major work on the subject. Two other excellent biographies by Tendulkar and Pyarelal, drawing extensively on Gandhi's own words, are cited in full on page 174. Both are available in inexpensive editions from Navajivan Publishing House, Ahmedabad-14, India.

The life of Abdul Ghaffar Khan deserves to be much better known around the world because it dispels the most common misunderstandings about nonviolence. The fullest biography to date, *Abdul Ghaffar Khan: Faith Is a Battle,* by D. G. Tendulkar (Bombay: Popular Prakashan, 1967), is difficult to find outside India; Eknath Easwaran has told Khan's story for the West in *A Man to Match His Mountains: Badshah Khan, Nonviolent Soldier of Islam* (Nilgiri Press, 1984).

APPLYING GANDHI'S IDEAS IN THE HOME

Gandhi's spiritual reference book, the Bhagavad Gita, is one of the most practical and profound works of mysticism in any language. *The Bhagavad Gita for Daily Living,* by Eknath Easwaran (Tomales, Calif.: Nilgiri Press, 1975–1988), was written for those who want to put the Gita into practice, as Gandhi did; the translation is contemporary and straightforward, and Easwaran has drawn freely on his experience to illustrate how each verse can be translated into everyday life. The same translation is available without the commentary, but with helpful introductions to the book and each chapter, as *The Bhagavad Gita* (Nilgiri Press, 1985).

For those who are interested in experimenting with their diet, there are several good vegetarian cookbooks available. *The New Laurel's Kitchen,* by Laurel Robertson, Carol Flinders, and Brian Ruppenthal (Ten Speed Press, 1986), is a comprehensive handbook for vegetarian cookery and nutrition compiled from Easwaran's perspective.

Acknowledgments

We are grateful to all who gave their permission to use photographs from their collections. Particularly generous were Lt.-Col. B. J. Bhatt (Ret.), Datta Khopker, Jagan V. Mehta, D. R. D. Wadia, Vithalbhai K. Jhaveri, and Mrs. Sumati Morarjee.

We would like especially to thank Navajivan Trust for its permission to quote from the following works by M. K. Gandhi:

All Men Are Brothers: Life and Thoughts of Mahatma Gandhi as Told in His Own Words, compiled and edited by Krishna Kripalani (Ahmedabad: Navajivan, 1960)

An Autobiography: The Story of My Experiments with Truth (Ahmedabad: Navajivan, 1940)

Gita–My Mother, edited and published by Anand K. Hingorani (Bombay: Bharatiya Vidya Bhavan, 1965)

Ramanama (Ahmedabad: Navajivan, 1949)

Selected Works, edited by Shriman Narayan (Ahmedabad: Navajivan, 1968). Vol. 3: *Satyagraha in South Africa* (first published 1928); vol. 5: *Selected Letters;* vol. 6: *The Voice of Truth*

Selections from Gandhi, edited by Nirmal Kumar Bose (Ahmedabad: Navajivan, 1957)

Navajivan also gave permission to use direct quotes from Gandhi from two excellent and comprehensive biographical studies: *Mahatma,* by D. G. Tendulkar (Bombay: Vithalbhai K. Jhaveri and D. G. Tendulkar, 1951) and *Mahatma Gandhi: The Early Phase,* by Pyarelal (Ahmedabad: Navajivan, 1956).

Index

Text references are indicated by the page numbers in roman type; italic page numbers refer to direct quotations from Gandhi in italics. References to photographs of persons or places are also included. Pronunciation and brief definitions are included for those Sanskrit words which might be unfamiliar to the reader. Vowels in Sanskrit are pronounced as follows: *a* as in *u*p, *ā* as in f*a*ther; *i* as in g*i*ve, *ī* as in s*ee*; *u* as in p*u*t, *ū* as in r*u*le; *e* as in th*ey*; *ai* as in *ai*sle; *o* as in g*o*; and *au* as in c*ow*. On the whole, the consonants may be pronounced as in English, except that an *h* is always pronounced: for example, the *bh* in Bhagavad Gita is pronounced as in a*bh*or. Accents have been added as an aid to pronunciation; they are indicated by ´.

Ábdul Gháffar Khan, 84; *photos*, *1*, *2*, *85*, *91*, *144*

Abdúlla, Dada, 21–22

Ahímsā ("nonviolence," completely selfless love), 53, 56, 89, 115, 151–54, 163, 166, 168, 169, 170; and truth, 153; definition of, 151–52; learning, 165; in personal relationships, 167–71. *See also* Love; Nonviolence; Satyagraha

Ambulance service, Gandhi's, 28, 36–37; *photo*, *29*

Anger, 122; harnessing, 36, 74

Arjuna, 35

Arrest, Gandhi's, 60, 70–71

Art of living, 121, 125

Áshram (community where spiritual disciplines are practiced), 28. *See also* Sabarmati ashram; Sevagram ashram

Assassination, Gandhi's, *100*, 140; attempted, 97

Bhāgavad Gítā, 34–36, 72, 84, *106*, *111*, *112*, 118, 119; summary of, 35; trans. of verses from 12th ch., "The Way of Love," 36; argues out law of love in scientific manner, *108*; trans. of verses from 2nd ch., describing perfect man or woman, *121–22*, 139

Bible, 72, 89, 139

Bihár. *See* Hindu-Muslim conflict

Birla, G. D., 149

Body an instrument of service, 137

Boycott, 148; of British cotton, 76

Bravery. *See* Fearlessness

British colonial rule, 11, 17, 49, 56, 60, 62, 67,
74, 76; end of, 164

British people, Gandhi wins over the, 74,
76, 81

Buddha, 53, 139, 170; his law of love, 97

Caste system. *See* Harijans

Childhood, Gandhi's, 11, *12*

Children, Gandhi's relationship with,
168–69

Churchill, Winston, 76

Civil disobedience, 43, 44, 70, 151, 158, 161; is
the right of a citizen, *43*. *See also*
Noncooperation; Satyagraha

Civil war in India. *See* Hindu-Muslim
conflict

College, Gandhi in, 16

Compromise, 155–56, 162–63

Conflict, nonviolent resolution of, 143, 157

Consciousness: transformation of, 33–34,
38, 84, 107, 145, 165–67; expansion of, 89,
126; unification of, 112, 115, 117–19, 121,
122, 140; summit of, 121, 122

Cooperation with opponent, 157–58

Cotton, British monopoly of, 76

Courage. *See* Fearlessness

Courtesy, 160, *164*

Creativity, the source of, 38

Dandi. *See* Salt March

Death, *97, 100, 122, 140;* Gandhi's, 140

Desai, Mahadev, 112, 139

Desires, unification of, 38, 112, 121

Detachment, *29,* 105–22 *passim;*
Gandhi's, during conflicts, 71, 72,
106, 133; his definition of, *105;*
in Gita, *111*

Devotion, *97*

Dharma (law of one's being), 56

Discipline, 149–150, 165

Eckhart, Meister, 125

Ends and means, 49, *105,* 151, 163

England, Gandhi in, 16–20 *passim,* 75–81,
112

Equal treatment of all, 35

Evolution: force behind, 38; summit of, 56,
121, 122

Experiments, Gandhi's: in food, 19, 137; in
art of living, 17, *142*

Exploitation, 46, 56, 60, 74

Family, the, 134–35; learning love in, 30–33,
125–26; practicing satyagraha in, 33–34,
125–26, 167–169

Fear: incompatible with nonviolence, *84,
87, 90;* Gandhi's, as a child, *12, 15,* 117

Fearlessness, 53, 84, *101, 115,* 116, 117

Fischer, Louis, 125, 135

Food, experiments with, 19, *137*

Force, spiritual, 38, 140, 152; satyagraha as,
148, 150, 165–66

Forgiveness, 84

Freedom, 106, 121; living for others makes
for, 28; steady mind leads to, 118

"Frontier Gandhi," *See* Abdul Ghaffar
Khan

Gandhi, Kásturbai (Gandhi's wife), 15, 30,
33; teaches him the way of love, 33–34,
125–26, 167–68; *photos, 14, 31, 32, 37, 127*

Gandhi, M. K.: childhood of, 11, *12,* 117;
marriage of, 15; in college, 16; as law
student in London, 17–20; as lawyer,
20–22; experiments of, in simple living,
19, *26, 28–30, 35;* begins to live for others,
25–30; learns nonviolence at home,
30–34, 125–26, 167–69; and
transformation of personality, *1,*
33–38, 105–22, 166–67; in South Africa,
36–38, 41–47, 166–67; and inspiration
for nonviolent resistance, 41, 43, 166;
presents challenge of satyagraha to

Gandhi, M. K. (*cont.*)
  India, 49; campaigns for Harijans,
    56–60; and transformation of others, 34,
    64–65, 84; begins nationwide satyagraha
    in India, 65–70; arrests of, 60, 70–71;
    trial of, 60, *62;* begins Salt Satyagraha,
    65–70; in jail, 72, 158; in England for
    Second Round Table Conference, 75–81,
    112, 147; and Pathans, 84; during Hindu-
    Muslim riots, 89–102; and cobra at
    prayer meeting, 115–16; daily life of,
    129–39; assassination of, 140; as living
    spiritual force, 140; and practice of
    nonviolence, 152–54; and children,
    168–69
George V, King of England, 76
God, *35, 89, 100, 105, 116,* 121, 122; leave all
    worry to Him, *29;* drawing nearer to
    Him, *117*

Hárijans ("Children of God": low-caste
    Hindus), Gandhi's campaigns for the,
    56, 59–60
Hatred, 53, 56, 97
Hindu-Muslim conflict, 89-102 *passim,*
    106, 140; *other photos,* 1, 2, 55
House of Commons, Gandhi speaks before
    the, 112
Humility, *112*

Ideal, Gandhi's, 36
Integration of consciousness. *See*
    Consciousness
Irwin, Lord, 70, 76

Jail, Gandhi in, 72, 75, *158–59*
Jones, Stanley, 75

Karma, law of, in Jesus' words, 56
Khádi (homespun cloth), 76
Khan Ábdul Gháffar Khan, 84; *photos,* 1, 2,
    85, 91, 144

Kripalani, J. B., 49
Krishna, Srī, 35
Kundalínī (evolutionary energy), 38

Lancashire, 76, 81
Lawyer, Gandhi as a, 20-25
Life, unity of. *See* Unity of life
Living, art of, 121, 125
Love, 53, 119, 121, *125, 126;* as root of
    nonviolence, 157; Gandhi defines true,
    89; law of, 97, 107, 147-48; learning, in
    marriage context, 15, 33-34, 125-26;
    satyagraha founded on, 147-48. *See also*
    Ahimsa; Nonviolence

Mantram (spiritual formula which
    transforms consciousness), 116, 117-18,
    122, 140
Maritzburg, Gandhi thrown off train at, 41;
    Gandhi's transformation at, 166
Marriage: Gandhi's, 15, 30-34, 125-26,
    167–68; practicing ahimsa in, 167-68
Meditation, 38, 72, 118-19
"Midnight arrest," Gandhi's, 70-71
Mill workers, 81
Mind, 122; calming the, 117-18. *See also*
    Peace of mind
Mother, Gandhi's, 16, 20
Muslim-Hindu conflict. *See* Hindu-
    Muslim conflict

Nehru, Jawáharlal, 64, 76, 133; *photos,* 63,
    132, 133
Nehru, Mótilal, 64–65
Noakháli. *See* Hindu-Muslim conflict
Noncooperation, 56, 60, *62,* 156, 157, 158,
    160. *See also* Satyagraha
Nonviolence, 50, 53, 74, *116,* 140, *142,* 151–54,
    171; and permanent solution of conflict,
    153; as way of life, 152–53; conversion of
    opponent through, 161; efficacy of, 154;
    Gandhi's decision to embrace, 41;

Nonviolence *(cont.)*

in family context, 33–34, 125–26, 167–69; in individual consciousness, 165; in personal relationships, 167–71; is force of love, 53; is law of human beings, 153; is real courage, 84; love is root of, 53, *156;* requires absolute fearlessness, *84, 90, 98, 101,* 115. *See also* Ahimsa; Satyagraha

Nonviolent resistance, 43, 70, 167–68. *See also* Civil disobedience

Nursing, 25, 28, 72, 134

Passive resistance, 150 , 160

Patánjali, 115

Pathans, 84

Patience, 167, 168

Peace of mind, *29, 112,* 122

Personality, the real, 115. *See also* Consciousness

Politics and religion, *60*

Porbándar, 11; *photo,* 10

Poor, the, 56–60, 62, 76, 81, *148*

Prayer, 38, *100. See also* Mantram; Meditation

Prayer meeting, 137, 139; cobra at, 115–116

Privacy, Gandhi's lack of, 131

Punctuality, Gandhi's, 132

Racial discrimination in South Africa, 21, 25, 41, 43

Ráma (Gandhi's mantram, a name of the Lord referring to inner power of joy). *See* Mantram

Reason, shortcomings of, 159, 160

Relationships, personal, satyagraha in, 167–69

Religion, 29, 34, 89; and politics, *60;* is the sum of one's life, *131*

Renunciation. *See* Detachment

Revolution, 64

Round Table Conference, Second, 75, 106, 112, 149; *photo,* 76–77

Sabármati áshram, 129

Salt March, 65–70, 166; *photos,* 49, 64, 66–67

Sanitary reform, 59

Satyágraha ("holding on to truth"; opposing injustice with love), 53, 147–51, 155–71; ahimsa is bedrock of, 151–52; and trust, 156–57; as spiritual force, 82, 148, 150, 152; compromise in, 162–63; cooperation with opponent in, 157–58; definition of, 48–49, 53, 147–50; discipline of, *54, 74,* 165; forms of, 148; flexibility of, 162, 171; in South Africa, 41–49, 148, *163,* 166; on family level, 167–69; on personal level, 164–67; reducing self-interest through, 165, 170–71; resolving conflict through, 147, 155, 164; role of suffering in, 157–58, 159–60, 161; success in, 163, 164; transformation of opponent through, 155–56, 157–58, 161, 164; truth and nonviolence as basis of, 53, 147–49, 151, 156, 162–63, 171; universal applicability of, 147, *151,* 164. *See also* Ahimsa; Love; Nonviolence; Nonviolent resistance

Satyágrahī (one who practices satyagraha), 53, *72,* 156–62, 170–71; and suffering, 157–58, 159–60, 161; courtesy of the, 161–62; Gandhi is first, 166; "weapons" of the, 157–58, 159–61

Self, the real, 115

Self-interest, reducing, 149–50, 165–67, 170–71. *See also* Zero: making oneself

Sermon on the Mount, 139; gives same message as Bhagavad Gita, *108*

Service, 22, 25, 28, 29

Sevagram áshram, 129; Gandhi's daily life at, 131–37

Sex, 38

Simple way of life, 17–19, 26, 28, *29, 30*

Smuts, Jan, 47, *157, 162*

South Africa, 21–49 *passim;* attitude toward Indians in, 155; racial discrimination in, 21, 25, 41, 43; satyagraha in, 41–49, 159, 163–64, 166–67

Spinning by hand, 76

Spontaneity, Gandhi's, 65–67

Strength, inner, 72, 87, 92

Success in satyagraha, 163–64, 166

Suffering, 25, 72, *149, 154;* in satyagraha, 157–58, 159–60, 161

Tolstoy Farm, 169

Transformation of consciousness. *See* Consciousness

Trial, Gandhi's, for sedition, 60; excerpts from his statement at, 62

Trust: building, in satyagraha, 53, 160–61, 163; in human nature, 53

Truth, *47,* 48–49, 53, *60,* 148–49, 164; Gandhi's search for, 17, 35, *142;* in satyagraha, *53,* 149, 156, 159, 162–63. *See also* Ahimsa; Nonviolence; Satyagraha

Unity of life, *31,* 53, 75, 114, *115,* 121, 156, 163, 170, 171

Upanishad, Íshá, 105

Vegetarianism, 19

Vegetarian Society, 20; *photo,* 18

Victory, 164, 165

Violence, *43, 54,* 105, 152, 153, 159, 164

Walking, 19, 117, 137

War, 38; within, the, 35–36, 89, 112

Weapons, a mark of cowardice or fear, 84

Weapons, nonviolent, 161

Will, *46, 87*

Woman, future of mankind is with, *134*

Work, 110; Gandhi's capacity for, 106; his daily, 131–37

Yerávda Central Prison, 72

Yoga (self-integration), 112

Zero: making oneself, *114,* 115, 149-50. *See also* Self-interest, reducing

Zulu "rebellion," 36, 38, 166